T0318801

China's Venture Capital Market

Elsevier
Asian Studies Series

Series Editor: Professor Chris Rowley,
Centre for Research on Asian Management, Cass Business School,
City University, UK; HEAD Foundation, Singapore
(email: *c.rowley@city.ac.uk*)

Elsevier is pleased to publish this major series of books entitled *Asian Studies: Contemporary Issues and Trends*. The Series Editor is Professor Chris Rowley, Director, Centre for Research on Asian Management, City University, UK and Director, Research and Publications, HEAD Foundation, Singapore.

Asia has clearly undergone some major transformations in recent years and books in the series examine this transformation from a number of perspectives: economic, management, social, political, and cultural. We seek authors from a broad range of areas and disciplinary interests covering, for example, business/management, political science, social science, history, sociology, gender studies, ethnography, economics, and international relations, etc.

Importantly, the series examines both current developments and possible future trends. The series is aimed at an international market of academics and professionals working in the area. The books have been specially commissioned from leading authors, with the objective of providing the reader with an authoritative view of current thinking.

New authors: we would be delighted to hear from you if you have an idea for a book. We are interested in both shorter, practically orientated publications (45,000+ words) and longer, theoretical monographs (75,000–100,000 words). Our books can be single, joint or multi-author volumes. If you have an idea for a book, please contact the publishers or Professor Chris Rowley, the series editor.

Professor Chris Rowley
Cass Business School, City University
Email: c.rowley@city.ac.uk
www.cass.city.ac.uk/faculty/c.rowley

Dr Glyn Jones
Email: g.jones.2@elsevier.com

China's Venture Capital Market

Current Legal Problems and Prospective Reforms

Lin Zhang

ELSEVIER

AMSTERDAM • BOSTON • HEIDELBERG • LONDON • NEW YORK • OXFORD
PARIS • SAN DIEGO • SAN FRANCISCO • SINGAPORE • SYDNEY • TOKYO

Elsevier
Radarweg 29, PO Box 211, 1000 AE Amsterdam, Netherlands
The Boulevard, Langford Lane, Kidlington, Oxford OX5 1GB, UK
225 Wyman Street, Waltham, MA 02451, USA

Notices
Knowledge and best practice in this field are constantly changing. As new research and experience broaden our understanding, changes in research methods, professional practices, or medical treatment may become necessary.

Practitioners and researchers must always rely on their own experience and knowledge in evaluating and using any information, methods, compounds, or experiments described herein. In using such information or methods they should be mindful of their own safety and the safety of others, including parties for whom they have a professional responsibility.

To the fullest extent of the law, neither the Publisher nor the authors, contributors, or editors, assume any liability for any injury and/or damage to persons or property as a matter of products liability, negligence or otherwise, or from any use or operation of any methods, products, instructions, or ideas contained in the material herein.

ISBN: 978-0-85709-450-6

British Library Cataloguing-in-Publication Data
A catalogue record for this book is available from the British Library

Library of Congress Cataloging-in-Publication Data
A catalog record for this book is available from the Library of Congress

Library of Congress Control Number: 2014955912

For information on all Elsevier publications
visit our website at http://store.elsevier.com/

Typeset by MPS Limited, Chennai, India
www.adi-mps.com

Printed and bound in United States of America

Dedication

山东省高校人文社会科学研究计划

Contents

List of tables		ix
About the author		xi
Preface		xiii
List of abbreviations		xv
1	**A profile of China's venture capital market**	**1**
	Venture capital and innovation	3
	A historical overview of the Chinese venture capital market	9
	A current profile of the Chinese venture capital market	20
2	**Fundraising for Chinese venture capital: legal problems and reform measures**	**25**
	A profile of fundraising for American venture capital	25
	Chinese pension funds	28
	Chinese commercial banks	32
	Chinese insurance companies	37
	Legal reform measures	41
3	**Operation of Chinese venture capital: legal problems and reform measures**	**45**
	Operation of American venture capital	45
	Operation of Chinese domestic venture capital	47
	Legal reform measures	51
4	**Exit of Chinese venture capital: legal problems and reform measures**	**53**
	Exit channels of American venture capital	53
	Exit channels of Chinese domestic venture capital	55
	Legal reform measures	60
5	**Conclusions: How long will it take for reform to take place in China?**	**63**
	Dispersal of the ownership of state-controlled listed companies	63
	Political reform in China	65
Notes		67
Bibliography		79
Index		83

List of tables

1.1   Total amount of venture capital under management in China between   21
2003 and 2006.

1.2   Annual amounts of venture capital investment in China between 2003   21
and 2006.

1.3   Differences in annual investment between domestic VCs and foreign   21
VCs in China, 2005 to 2007.

1.4   Differences in total registered capital between domestic VC institutions   22
and foreign VC institutions in China, 2005 to 2007.

2.1   Summary of statistics for venture capital fundraising in America, 1978   27
to 2002.

2.2   Social security funds in China.   31

4.1   An overview of listed companies on the SME Board of the Shenzhen   58
Stock Exchange, 2004 to 2007.

4.2   Numbers of listed companies on the SME Board of the Shenzhen Stock   59
Exchange, 2004 to 2007.

About the author

Lin Zhang has been an assistant professor at Korea University School of Law since September 2012. He obtained his PhD in commercial law from the University of Hong Kong in 2010. In addition, he was admitted to the Chinese Bar in 2008 and has been a part-time corporate lawyer in a leading Chinese law firm, headquartered in Beijing, since 2010. His primary research interests include commercial law, international economic law, and Chinese law.

During the past five years, he has authored two monographs, published by Springer and Elsevier respectively. He has also produced a number of high-caliber research articles, which have been included in blindly-refereed law journals in the US, the UK, Switzerland, South Korea, and China. He can be contacted at linzhang@korea.ac.kr.

Preface

In 1984, on the basis of findings reported by a project entitled 'New Technology and China's Countermeasures', the Chinese National Centre of Science and Technology for Development put forth the suggestion that a venture capital system should be engineered in order to promote technological development in China. This proposal quickly drew attention from the Central Committee of the CPC and the Chinese Central Government, marking the inception of Chinese venture capital. By the end of 2006, China had become the second biggest venture capital market in the world, behind only America.

History, however, records both achievements and problems. With regard to Chinese venture capital, it would be overoptimistic to believe that the development of venture capital has followed an exclusively upward trajectory. Thus, an important task in this field lies in determining what problems have arisen from the booming of the Chinese venture capital market.

Existing statistics suggest that Chinese domestic venture capital has been marginalized by its foreign competitors. This book attempts to address this weakness by examining the negative role played by the legal system in the formation of the competitive weaknesses of Chinese domestic venture capital as compared with its foreign rivals. In addition, legal reform measures which could remedy the situation are proposed.

This book could not have been completed without the support I received from multiple sources. First of all, I am grateful to my wife Ann and my son Johnson for their selfless love and understanding. In addition, I am obliged to Springer for generously allowing me to draw on materials from my last monograph, entitled 'Venture Capital and the Corporate Governance of Chinese Listed Companies'. Last, but not least, I am indebted to the ICR Center of Korea University and the Ecological Civilization and Economic Development Center of Shandong Province ("山东省生态文明与经济社会发展科研基地学术基金资助") for their financial sponsorship of this book.

List of abbreviations

AIG	American International Group
ARDC	American Research Development Corporation
BVI	British Virgin Islands
China Life	China Life Insurance Company
CNTVIC	China New Technology Venture Investment Corporation
COSHIP	COSHIP Electronics Companies
CPC	Communist Party of China
CSRC	China Securities Regulatory Commission
CTTIC	CTTIC Group Corporation
DEC	Digital Equipment Corporation
ERISA	Employee Retirement Income Security Act
Fortune Capital	Shenzhen Fortune Capital Company
GEM	Growth Enterprise Market
Govtor Capital	Jiangsu Govtor Capital Company
HTBIC	Hunan TV & Broadcast Intermediary Company
Insurance Law	Insurance Law of the PRC
Jiangsu Venture Fund	Jiangsu Technology Development Venture Fund
KMT	Kuomingtang
LCDs	Liquid Crystal Displays
Microsoft	Microsoft Corporation
MOC	Ministry of Commerce
MOF	Ministry of Finance
NASDAQ	National Association of Securities Dealers Automated Quotations
Ningxiahong Group	Ningxiahong Wolfberry Industry Group
Partnership Law	Partnership Enterprise Law of the PRC
PICC	People's Insurance Company of China
Ping An Company	Ping An Insurance (Group) Company of China
SAFE	State Administration of Foreign Currency
SAIC	State Administration for Industry and Commerce
SAT	State Administration of Taxation
SEC	Securities and Exchange Commission
SME Board	Small and Medium-sized Enterprise Board

SOE	State-owned Enterprises
SPDB	Shanghai Pudong Development Bank
SPVs	Special Purpose Vehicles
SSF	National Council for Social Security Fund
SSTC	State Scientific and Technological Commission
Sun	Nailiang Sun
SVB	Silicon Valley Bank
Xiangshan Company	Ningxia Xiangshan Liquor Company
Xiangshan Wolfberry Company	Ningxia Xiangshan Zhongning Wolfberry Products Company
Zhang	Jinshan Zhang
Zhongning Firm	Zhongning Wolfberry Preserves Firm
Zhongwei Firm	Ningxia Zhongwei Liquor Firm
1991 Decision	Decision of the State Council to Reform the Pension Scheme of SOEs

A profile of China's venture capital market

In 1946, with the generous support of Ralph Flanders and MIT President Karl Compton, General Georges Doriot, then a professor of industrial management at Harvard Business School, established the first modern venture capital firm in the United States of America. Named American Research Development Corporation (ARDC), the mission of the new firm was simple but far-reaching: '…aid in the development of new or existing businesses into companies of stature and importance.' During its 26-year existence, ARDC's most notable success resulted from its decision to put up $70,000 to support Kenneth Olsen and Harlan Anderson in founding Digital Equipment Corporation (DEC). In its first year, DEC recorded a small profit by producing Digital Laboratory Modules, but the real harvest occurred dozens of years later. In 1968, in the wake of DEC's successful initial public offering, the value of ARDC's stake quickly grew to $355 million.[1]

ARDC was only the beginning of the success story of American venture capital. In 1978, the US Labor Department undid some of the restrictions of the Employee Retirement Income Security Act (ERISA), known as the 'prudent man rule', thus allowing pension funds to inject a tremendous amount of money into American venture capital firms. Following that decision, the American venture capital industry entered a 'golden age' lasting until the year 2000.[2] During its boom period, American venture capital incubated many companies which have become household names, such as Microsoft, Apple, and Lotus, and paved the way for America to become the unparalleled leader in the global high-technology market.[3] Even though the bursting of the Internet bubble tainted its image in 2000, American venture capital continues to be considered the 'jewel in the crown' of the American economy, and the engine which continues to push it forward.[4]

The legend of American venture capital has inspired the ambitions of other major economic powers, as well as emerging economies throughout the world, to engineer their own vibrant venture capital markets. The past several decades have witnessed such efforts in Europe, the Middle East, and Asia.[5] Some of these endeavors have turned out rather successfully, while others have ended in failure.[6] Regardless of results in individual countries, however, the trend represented by these attempts as a whole indicates that a consensus on the significance of a vibrant venture capital market has been reached by countries all over the world.

Relative to its American counterpart, the growth of China's venture capital market has been through many more hardships. Soon after the inception of the People's Republic of China in 1949, the Communist Party of China (CPC) launched a movement to nationalize privately-held enterprises.[7] By the end of 1956, this movement led to the establishment of a state-owned economy in China, which was characterized by the pervasiveness of state-owned enterprises (SOEs).[8] In addition, consistent with the dominance of a state-owned economy, the CPC replicated the centrally-planned approach of the former Soviet Union to manage production and allocate resources in the country.[9] The existence of the centrally-planned system completely suppressed the appearance of any substantive elements of the market-oriented economy. Consequently, venture capital was excluded from China's economy for a long period of time.

Since 1978, China's economic ship has been steered by the policy of reform and opening-up which aims to transform China's economy from a centrally-planned one to a market-oriented one, as defined by Mr. Xiaoping Deng, the principal architect of the transition. In the midst of this continuous institutional change, salient features of the market-oriented economy have been gradually emerging and becoming well-established in China, such as the 'invisible hand' of pricing, privatization of SOEs, and the venture capital with which this book is concerned.

In 1984, based on the findings of a project entitled 'New Technology and China's Countermeasures', the Chinese National Centre of Science and Technology for Development put forth the suggestion that a venture capital system should be engineered in order to promote technological development in China.[10] This proposal quickly drew attention from the Central Committee of the CPC and the Chinese Central Government. In 1985, the CPC Central Committee promulgated its 'Decisions to Reform the Science and Technology System', in which the reigning party recognized for the first time the supportive role of venture capital in developing high-quality technologies.[11] Only one year after this positive signal from the CPC on venture capital, the first Chinese venture capital firm, China New Technology Venture Investment Corporation, was established jointly by the State Science and Technology Committee and the Ministry of Finance, a move symbolizing the bourgeon of the Chinese venture capital market. Since then, the development of venture capital in China has gone through several landmark stages.[12] By the end of 2006, China had become the second biggest venture capital market in the world, behind only America.

History, however, records both achievements and problems, a principle which ought to be applied to the observation of any phenomenon in the mundane world. With regard to China's venture capital market, it would be overoptimistic to believe that it has followed an exclusively upward trajectory. Taking this attitude would blind us to the realities of the situation. A better approach would be to observe the problems, both past and present, in China's venture capital sector. Identifying these problems is the first step in subsequent efforts to determine their underlying causes. This book concentrates on legal factors, although there are undoubtedly other relevant factors.

This chapter is comprised of three parts. Given the close association between venture capital and innovation, the first part analyzes the role of venture capital in promoting a country's innovative ability, which was also the inspiration behind the CPC's initial decision to engineer China's venture capital market. The second part provides an overview of the historical stages in the development of China's venture capital market. Finally, the third part describes the current profile of the Chinese venture capital market. This description, together with the historical overview in the second part, illustrates the problems currently suffered by China's venture capital market. Between them, these parts constitute the context in which the remaining chapters of the book unfold: the search for the underlying legal causes of these problems.

Venture capital and innovation

By definition, innovation is the creation of better or more effective products, processes, services, technologies, or ideas. Innovation is usually classified into two categories: in-house innovation and external innovation.[13] In-house innovation typically occurs in large, well-established firms and existing industries.[14] External innovation, by contrast, generally takes place in startups set up by entrepreneurs.[15] These startups have impacts not only on existing industries, but also on the creation of entirely new industries. The propensity of venture capital towards financing high technology start-ups determines that it plays an essential role in promoting external innovation. Rather than relying on obscure statistics, three case studies will be related below as a vivid way to illustrate the link between venture capital and external innovation.

Case study: Facebook[16]

Facebook was initially founded in 2004 by Mark Zuckerberg, then a Harvard junior, with his college roommates and fellow students Eduardo Saverin, Dustin Moskovitz, and Chris Hughes. At first, membership of the website was available only to Harvard students, but it was gradually extended to other universities and colleges in the Boston area, the Ivy League, and Stanford University. Later, Facebook was also opened to students at various other universities prior to granting eligibility to high school students, and eventually to anyone aged 13 or above. In January 2009, it was reported that Facebook was ranked as the most used social networking service provider.

In the process of realizing the miracle of Facebook, venture capital played an important role. In late 2004, Facebook received its first venture capital investment, $500,000, from Peter Andreas Thiel, a venture capitalist and co-founder of PayPal. In 2005, Jim Breyer, a venture capitalist with Accel Partners, formed a wonderful impression of Mark Zuckerberg upon meeting him. Soon afterwards, Breyer invested $1,500,000 in the promising social network provider. As Breyer said at the time: 'it is a business that has seen tremendous underlying, organic growth and the team itself is intellectually honest and breathtakingly brilliant in terms of understanding the college student experience'. In 2006, Greylock Partners, which is one of the oldest and most famous venture capital firms in America, led a $27,500,000 investment into Facebook with several other investors. At first, given Facebook's unpredictable future, this was deemed to be an extremely risky investment. Subsequent tremendous profits from the venture, however, demonstrated that Greylock Partners had made a very sensible decision. This also stabilized Greylock's status in Silicon Valley as a magnate investor in Web 2.0 startups. Using these first three rounds of financing from venture capital, Facebook quickly grew to become a rising star in the field of social networking services. Since then, it has begun to attract attention from gigantic firms. In 2007, Facebook officially announced that it had sold out 1.6 per cent of its shares to Microsoft Corporation (Microsoft) for $240,000,000. Following the establishment of this partnership with Microsoft, in 2009, Facebook received another investment, worth $200,000,000, from Digital Sky Technologies, a prominent Internet investor in Russia and Europe. Looking back at the financing of Facebook over the past several years, it is fair to say that venture capital has been a key factor in establishing the leading position of Facebook in the social media sector. Furthermore, the success of Facebook has generated breakthrough impacts on several dimensions of society, further connecting venture capital with innovation. These impacts are listed below.

Impact on advertisement

In April 2011, a new portal was officially launched by Facebook with the aim of providing a platform for market developers to promote their brands. Along with its continuous push to attract more advertisement, Facebook currently features an online voting poll for the most popular television shows such as True Blood, American Idol, and Top Gear. Influential news and media agencies such as the Washington Post, Financial Times, and ABC News have also used Facebook as a channel to collect opinions, comments and feedback from their audiences.

Impact on daily life

Facebook has affected the daily life and activity of people in various ways. With its compatibility with many mobile devices, Facebook allows members to continuously keep in touch with families, friends, and other contacts wherever they are in the world, as long as they have access to the Internet. It can also bring together individuals with common interests, backgrounds, experience, and beliefs through its groups, and has been credited with reuniting lost family members and friends due to the broad reach of its network. As revealed by Wiki, 'one such reunion was between John Watson and the daughter he had been seeking for 20 years. They met after Watson found her Facebook profile. Another father-daughter reunion was between Tony Macnauton and Frances Simpson, who had not seen each other for nearly 48 years'.

Impact on political life

The American presidential election in 2008 was the first in which all candidates attempted to connect directly with American voters via online social networking sites such as Facebook. As a result of this, it has even been called the 'Facebook election'. The extent of these online endeavors by candidates is effectively demonstrated by the fact that one of Barack Obama's key strategists was Chris Hughes, one of the co-founders of Facebook. As U.S. News remarked, 'it was Hughes who masterminded the Obama campaign's highly effective Web blitzkrieg—everything from social networking sites to podcasting and mobile messaging'.

Facebook was also quick to realize its suddenly influential role in American political life. During the 2008 presidential campaign, the social networking provider opened up its own forum to encourage online debates about electoral issues. It also teamed up with ABC for election coverage. The victory of President Obama can be seen as evidence that Facebook has become an integral part of American politics and democracy, because '[Obama] was the first occupant of the White House to have won a presidential election on the Web'.

Impact on popular culture

The widespread reach of Facebook has also accelerated the appearance of pop figures and broadened the scope of pop culture. The story of Ivy Bean, which is included in Wiki and quoted below, is a convincing example in this regard.

> *At age 102, Ivy Bean of Bradford, England joined Facebook in 2008, making her one of the oldest people ever on Facebook. An inspiration to other residents of the care home in which she lived, she quickly became more widely known and several fan pages were made in her honor. She visited then British Prime Minister Gordon Brown and his wife, Sarah, in Downing Street early in 2010. Some time after creating her Facebook page, Bean joined Twitter, when she passed the maximum number of friends allowed by Facebook. She became the oldest person to ever use the Twitter Web site. At the time of her death in July 2010, she had 4,962 friends on Facebook and more than 56,000 followers on Twitter. Her death was widely reported in the media and she received tributes from several notable media personalities.*

Case study: Alibaba[17]

Jack Ma, the founder of Alibaba, was once an English teacher at a Chinese university located in Hangzhou of Zhejiang Province. During his teachership, Jack established the first English translation agency in Hangzhou. In 1995, Jack was commissioned by Zhejiang Transportation Bureau to meet one of its debtors in Seattle. The meeting turned out to be a failure, but Jack came into contact with the Internet for the first time in his life. During his several days in Seattle, Jack tentatively posted an advertisement on the Internet to promote his translation agency. To his surprise, within two hours he received six emails from Internet users in America, Japan, and Germany. This attempt caused Jack to realize the huge potential for connection through the Internet. Meanwhile, an idea occurred to him that it could be profitable to design a website to aggregate the advertisement of Chinese enterprises to the outside world.

Back in Hangzhou from Seattle, Jack quickly converted his idea into action. With one of his friends and his wife, Jack set up his first Internet company. Named 'Hai Bo Network', it was focused on providing China's online yellow book. The venture achieved big success, with a turnover of more than RMB 7 million in its first year of operation. Overnight, Jack became an iconic figure in the country.

Jack's innovations didn't end with the success of Hai Bo Network, however. For him, China's online yellow book was only the start of his ambitions. Next, he aspired to develop the e-commerce market in China. In 1998, Jack launched a B2B e-commerce website called 'Alibaba'. In the 14 years since its inception, Alibaba has become a leader and giant in the field of B2B e-commerce. During the process, venture capital has also played an essential role, as explained below.

The first round of fundraising between Alibaba and venture capital occurred on 26 October 1999. Goldman Sachs, along with Transpac, Singapore TDF, Investor AB and Fidelity, injected $5 million into Alibaba to support its expansion and further development. In addition, in the process of the fundraising, Chongxin Cai, Asian representative of Investor AB, realized the huge potential of Alibaba and made a decision to resign from Investor AB and join the young company as its CFO, contributing valuable intellectual strength to the fast growth of Alibaba. The second fundraising contract was made between Alibaba and SoftBank Corporation, a prominent venture capital agency in the field of IT, on 17 January 2000. Zhengyi Sun, chairman of SoftBank Corporation, greatly appreciated the talents of Jack and the brand new idea of Alibaba after meeting him in Beijing and Tokyo in October 1999, and quickly and generously put up $20 million to fund the growth of the enterprise. More importantly, together with the investment, Zhengyi Sun officially became the chief consultant of Alibaba. Besides money, his joining has also brought reputation capital and an innovative strategic approach to the development of Alibaba. The third round of fundraising for Alibaba was undertaken with JAIC International in February 2002. In this round, Alibaba acquired $5 million from JAIC International to promote its market development in Japan. Around two years after the third round of fundraising, Alibaba went through a fourth round of fundraising. On 17 February 2004, Alibaba officially announced that it had successfully obtained a strategic investment of $82 million jointly from SoftBank Corporation, Fidelity, Singapore TDF, and Granite Global Ventures. This huge amount of money was used to facilitate the futuristic innovation of Alibaba in the area of e-commerce.

With the continuous support of venture capital Alibaba, as the pioneer of China's e-commerce, has changed the traditional business model in several ways. These changes are summarized below.

Information flow

One feature of a traditional business model is that sellers must rely on physical stores to provide information about their commodities to customers. In other words, under this model, sellers have to purchase or rent their own physical stores to showcase their goods to consumers. Maintaining a decent store, however, is usually associated with additional, sometimes considerable, costs. By launching an electronic advertising platform, Alibaba has overcome this shortcoming of the traditional business model. With this e-platform, sellers need only register for a free Alibaba user account and advertise their commodities on the platform. This kind of e-commerce model removes sellers' dependence on physical stores and reduces their operational costs. In addition, through making use of the vast connective power of the Internet, sellers can spread information about their commodities to many more customers all over the world.

Value-added service

Besides launching an e-commerce platform, Alibaba also plays the role of the intermediary, providing credit information to both sellers and customers through its value-added service. Under a traditional business model, a seller generally has to bear high transaction costs to check the credit background of potential customers, especially when the customers are individuals or small enterprises. By paying a relatively low annual fee to Alibaba, however, sellers purchase the privilege of requesting accurate credit information about their potential customers from the platform. In addition, after paying the annual fee, sellers are also entitled to display their credit certificates on

Alibaba's platform, verifying their credentials and lowering the information costs of customers. Therefore, the value-added service of Alibaba reduces transaction costs for both sellers and customers.

Payment platform

In addition to its innovative approach to proliferating information, Alibaba has also led a revolution in payment. Under a traditional business model, it is common practice for sellers to dispatch goods to customers only after they receive full or partial payment. For customers, this model means that they risk losing their money due to fraudulent salesmanship. Undoubtedly, victims of fraud may turn to courts or arbitrators for redress, but litigation or arbitration involves further costs. Thus, in order to lower the risk for customers, Alibaba has designed a payment platform entitled 'Alipay'. Once they open an Alipay account, sellers may ask customers to pay money into this account. Then, this amount of money is under the trust of Alibaba. After customers receive their goods and verify the quality, they instruct Alibaba to transfer payment into the sellers' hands. Hence, Alipay guarantees the security of transactions between sellers and customers.

Case study: Ningxiahong[18]

Ningxiahong Wolfberry Industry Group (Ningxiahong Group) arose from Ningxia Zhongwei Liquor Firm (Zhongwei Firm), a former SOE. After 40 years' development, Zhongwei Firm was confronted with a crisis of insolvency in 1996, due to its weak innovative ability, outdated technologies, and lax management. In order to rescue this moribund enterprise, local officials invited Jinshan Zhang (Zhang) to take over Zhongwei Firm. Zhang accepted the invitation of the local government and quickly incorporated Zhongwei Firm under the new name of 'Ningxia Xiangshan Liquor Company' (Xiangshan Company).

In 1997, only one year after its incorporation, Xiangshan Company successfully escaped from losses and made satisfactory profits. By 1998, another year later, it had claimed a 60 per cent share of the liquor market in Ningxia Province and become a famous local brand. This first-stage success did not satisfy Zhang, however, because he saw clearly that Xiangshan Company would always be a local name in the Chinese liquor market, as compared with Maotai or Wu Liangye, which are nationally prestigious brands. Thus, he concluded that Xiangshan Company must find another way to achieve breakthrough successes.

In his search for a new direction, Zhang first considered entering the wine market. Given the large quantity of grapes grown in Ningxia Province, it is fair to say that this idea was worth investigating. Following a thorough market survey, however, Zhang rejected it. As a result of the survey, he realised that China's wine market was close to being monopolized by several giant Chinese wine companies, such as Chang Yu, Greatwall, and Dynasty. Hence, he believed that entering the wine market would be a poor choice, based only on the grape advantages of Ningxia Province, not on an understanding of the market.

After giving up on squeezing into China's wine market, Zhang transferred his attention to another widely-planted but geographically unique plant of Ningxia Province: wolfberries. Wolfberries are a common plant with a planting history of more than 500 years on the Ningxia Plain. Although they also grow in other provinces of China, only the wolfberries from Ningxia Province are edible and nutritious for geographical reasons. Local inhabitants of the Ningxia Plain have been adding wolfberries to liquor for many years. According to scientific research, however, this kind of primitive use of wolfberries can only release 10 per cent of their intrinsic nutrition. Reflecting on this situation, an idea suddenly came into Zhang's mind: he would fill a market gap by producing an alcoholic liquor brewed with wolfberries.

Coincidently, as the above idea was occurring to Zhang, Zhongning Wolfberry Preserves Firm (Zhongning Firm) was on the brink of bankruptcy. Zhang seized this valuable opportunity by swiftly acquiring Zhongning Firm and then incorporating it under the new name of 'Ningxia Xiangshan Zhongning Wolfberry Products Company' (Xiangshan Wolfberry Company). Next, as a result of Zhang's efforts, Xiangshan Wolfberry Company established partnerships with several famous brewing technology research institutes in China to jointly develop a wolfberry liquor. In 2001, the brand new liquor, bearing the geographically-specific name 'Ningxiahong', entered the market.

The appearance of Ningxiahong quickly attracted the attention of Actis Capital, a reputable venture capital agency focusing principally on emerging markets. By analyzing China's alcohol market at that time, Actis Capital believed that the new concept of Ningxiahong would begin to generate profits in the not-too-distant future. Therefore, in September 2004, it announced an investment of $10 million into Ningxiahong. The participation of Actis Capital not only offered abundant finances for the product innovation of Ningxiahong, but also contributed valuable non-monetary inputs to the endeavor. These are summarized below.

Management advice

Prior to the investment of Actis Captial, the successful development of Ningxiahong was largely ascribed to the outstanding managerial ability of Zhang. Excepting this, Ningxiahong had not possessed a strong team consisting of professional managers to support its sustainable innovation and development. In order to remedy this disadvantage, soon after its investment, Actis Capital helped Ningxiahong successfully recruit a beverage expert as its director. The expert once worked for Coca-Cola and had thus accumulated rich experience in beverage products. Therefore, his presence strengthened Ningxiahong's ability to extend further into the beverage market.

Technological support

Actis Capital also made use of its network to seek technological support for Ningxiahong. For example, in 2004, Ningxiahong purchased two filling lines worth RMB 30 million from Italy. After they were installed in the Ningxiahong factory, however, the two filling lines could not run stably. After hearing of the situation, Actis Capital quickly invited two senior technicians from Coca-Cola to check and repair the two filling lines. It took these two technicians only a few days to resolve the bug, and Ningxiahong paid only RMB 3000 for the repair service.

Listing consultancy

It is Zhang's ambition that Ningxiahong will someday be listed on the Hong Kong Stock Exchange. His strategic co-operation with Actis Capital has provided useful assistance in achieving this dream as soon as possible. Before investing in Ningxiahong, Actis Capital exited profitably from Mengniu, which eventually accomplished its IPO on the Hong Kong Stock Exchange on 10 June 2004, with the assistance of Actis Capital and other venture capital agencies. Hence, Actis Capital has experience of incubating an enterprise from a seed to a listed star.

Since making its investment, Actis Capital has begun to consult with Ningxiahong on restructuring its ownership, improving its corporate governance, and strengthening its financial conditions. As a result of this consultation, progress towards listing Ningxiahong on the stock market has been accelerated.

To sum up, the above three cases of Facebook, Alibaba, and Ningxiahong illustrate how venture capital nurtures the growth of small companies representing external innovation from the startup stage to becoming big names in their respective markets. The success of these three companies has already significantly changed our lives. While we enjoy the convenience resulting from these changes, however, we should remember the hero behind the scenes; venture capital.

A historical overview of the Chinese venture capital market

Up to now, the development of the Chinese venture capital market has consisted of three stages. The first stage took place between 1984 and 1990, after the Chinese Central Government started its pilot trial to engineer a venture capital market in China. The second stage, in which Chinese local governments begun to play a significant role in the endeavor of establishing China's venture capital market, lasted from 1990 until 1998. The third stage, which has witnessed the fast-tracking of Chinese venture capital, mainly due to the participation of foreign venture capital, covers the period from 1998 until the present day. Next, the three stages will be elaborated upon one by one.

The first stage (1984–1990)

In 1984, based on the findings of a project named 'New Technology and China's Countermeasures', the National Centre of Science and Technology for Development put forth the suggestion that a venture capital market should be engineered in order to promote technological development in China.[19] This proposal quickly drew the attention of the CPC Central Committee and the Chinese Central Government. In 1985, the CPC Central Committee promulgated its 'Decision to Reform the Science and Technology System', in which the reigning party first recognized the supportive role of venture capital in developing high-quality technologies.[20] Echoing the positive attitude of the CPC Central Committee toward the initiative, the Chinese Central Government subsequently took a series of measures to kickstart the Chinese venture capital market during this period. Among these measures were the incorporation of China New Technology Venture Investment Corporation (CNTVIC) and the launching of the Torch Scheme.

China New Technology Venture Investment Corporation[21]

The CNTVIC was incorporated in January 1986 with registered capital of RMB 40 million. Its principal shareholders included State Scientific and Technological Commission (SSTC), the Ministry of Finance (MOF), and CTTIC Group Corporation (CTTIC). Since its inception, the CNTVIC has been viewed as China's first venture capital agency. Its mission has been to support potentially promising high-technology startups by means of equity investment, loans, guarantees, and several other financial services.

In its early stages, the CNTVIC focused primarily on incubating high-technology startups. In its first year, 1986, for example, the CNTVIC reviewed more than 200 business proposals and finally made a total investment of RMB 47.735 million into 65 of them. The investee companies operated mainly in the fields of information technology, biological technology, new materials, and circuits, all of which are technology-intensive sectors. In its second year, 1987, the CNTVIC continued to enlarge its investment into high-technology startups. That year, its total investment grew from RMB 47.735 million to RMB 170 million. The concentration of the young CNTVIC on technological development quickly reaped rewards. For instance, the CNTVIC put up RMB 6.85 million for the expansion of several high-technology startups in Jiangsu Province. After only one year, the overall turnover of these companies increased to RMB 100 million. On the basis of a series of successful investments into high-technology ventures, funds under the management of the CNTVIC had expanded to nearly RMB 2 billion by the end of 1990.

The CNTVIC, however, appeared in the context of China's initial transition from a centrally-planned economy to a market-oriented one. At that time, there seemed to be several other burgeoning markets in China which might provide the chance to make fast bucks, such as the stock market and the real estate market. Consequently, these potential opportunities gradually enticed the management of the CNTVIC away from venture capital. For example, the CNTVIC put up huge money to purchase stocks and develop the emerging real estate market of Hainan Province after 1990. More worryingly, most of the money was raised by taking deposits from the public at high interest rates. Therefore, there was a tremendous risk that the CNTVIC would default on its repayment obligation to depositors when investments into stocks and real estate suffered big losses. In addition, at that time, corporate governance and internal control were still novel concepts to Chinese companies. The CNTVIC was no exception. The lack of well-devised monitoring mechanisms led to a series of scandals which tainted the reputation of the CNTVIC and accelerated its demise. From April 1996 to October 1997, for example, Nailiang Sun (Sun), who was deputy manager of the trust department of the CNTVIC during the above period, embezzled RMB 20 million into his own company and another RMB 9.5 million for his own stock purchase. Even though the amount of money appropriated by him was huge, the primitive monitoring mechanisms of the CNTVIC did not spot Sun's illegal behavior in a timely manner. The deviation from venture capital, combined with porous corporate governance, eventually pushed the CNTVIC to its end with debts of RMB 6 billion total in 1998.

The operations and ultimate failure of the CNTVIC reflected the features of Chinese companies in that period of time. On the one hand, the majority of so-called 'Chinese companies' at the beginning of the 1990s were de facto SOEs growing from the previous centrally-planned economy. Therefore, they still operated from a belief common to that time; namely that the business interests of a sound SOE should be diverse. In the context of such a business culture, it is not difficult to understand why the CNTVIC, as an SOE, deviated from the field of venture capital and invested substantially in other financial sectors which were beyond the mission of its incorporation. The past, however, tells us that a company usually fails when it attempts to operate in multiple business arenas. Equally, SOEs in China at that time may have called themselves 'companies', but their governance frameworks were not restructured to emulate those of modern business corporations. Instead, they continued to follow the bureaucratic procedures prevalent in the centrally-planned economy to make investment decisions and monitor business activities. Consistent with sluggish central planning at the national level, bureaucratic procedure at the enterprise level was also lax and unresponsive. Consequently, a member of an SOE could easily cover illegal behavior for a long time by making use of the defects of the porous monitoring system. Usually, misconduct would not be spotted until it had led to tremendous losses to the SOE. Therefore, the case of Nailiang Sun in such a context was not exceptional but inevitable for the CNTVIC.

The Torch Scheme[22]

Apart from establishing the venture capital agencies affiliated to it, the Chinese Central Government also searched for other approaches to quickly engineer a venture capital market in China in the late 1980s. At that time, in the opinion of senior officials in the Chinese Central Government who were in charge of the development of venture capital, setting up venture capital agencies at the state level was essential but not sufficient, because the fiscal revenue of the Chinese Central Government could not satisfy the monetary demands of high technology startups all over the country. Therefore, there had to be another approach parallel to the CNTVIC model to boost the enthusiasm of local governments for participating in the endeavor. The overnight sensation of Zhongguancun Science Park offered the Chinese Central Government precisely such an idea.

In 1980, in a street in Zhongguancun, Beijing, several scientists from the Institute of Physical Sciences, part of the Chinese Academy of Sciences, established the first high technology startup in communist China, entitled 'Beijing Advanced Technology Service Agency'. Subsequently, a number of similar enterprises appeared in the same street and elsewhere in the neighborhood. In 1987, a team led by Jiabao Wen, who is currently China's Premier, conducted a survey on this cluster of high technology start-ups. On the basis of their findings, Jiabao Wen and his team suggested that the Central Committee of the CPC and the Chinese Central Government approve the establishment of a high technology zone in the Zhongguancun area, modeled on Silicon Valley. Their suggestion was quickly adopted by the supreme authority. On 20 May 1985, with the authorization of the Chinese Central Government, Beijing Municipal Government released the 'Provisional Regulation of Beijing High Technology Development Area', which declared the official opening of Zhongguancun Science Park. Pursuant to this regulation the Chinese Central Government offered a package of benefits, including taxation, foreign currency, accounting, loans, employment, and so on, to the high technology startups residing in Zhongguancun Science Park. The advent of Zhongguancun Science Park quickly drew the attention of other provinces, which appealed to the Chinese Central Government to approve the establishment of similar high technology zones in their own regions. With the unexpected popularity of the concept of 'high technology zones' with local governments, the Chinese Central Government realized that it had discovered a decentralized approach to building China's venture capital market. For the Chinese Central Government itself, the new approach consisted of two steps. First, the Chinese Central Government helped local governments to build up their own high technology zones modeled on Zhongguancun Science Park, through offering them financial support and policy benefits. Secondly, once they were in place, the development of high technology zones was incorporated into the responsibilities of local senior officials, and they were assessed on their performance in this regard. The establishment of venture capital funds by local governments in these zones was seen as a key indicator. Thus, local governments were incentivized to develop venture capital funds. The Torch Scheme was launched by the Chinese Central Government in August 1988.

On 6 August 1988, the first Torch Scheme working meeting was held in Beijing. During the meeting, Xuer Li, then vice director of the SSTC, announced that the Torch Scheme was to be officially implemented from that day onwards. The principle mission of the Scheme was, and continues to be, to process the applications of local governments wishing to establish their own high technology zones, and offer financial sponsorship and policy benefits to those whose applications were approved. Under the auspices of the Torch Scheme, another seven high technology zones, located in different regions to Zhongguancun Science Park, were opened by the end of 1988. Thus far, more than 90 such zones have been established throughout the country.

To sum up, both the CNTVIC and the Torch Scheme reflected the state-dominated nature of China's venture capital market in its embryonic stages. The CNTVIC model represented the direct involvement of the Chinese Central Government, through the investment of its own fiscal revenues into high technology startups. Contrastingly, the Torch Scheme exemplified the attempts of the Chinese Central Government to find a decentralized approach to fast-tracking China's venture capital market. Along with the implementation of high technology zones sponsored by the Torch Scheme, the Chinese venture capital market moved into its second stage when local governments played a leading role.

The second stage (1991–1997)

On 6 March 1991, the Chinese Central Government promulgated a regulation entitled 'Provisional Regulation on the Policies of National High Technology Development Zones', in which local governments were encouraged to set up venture capital funds or even incorporate venture capital companies in their own high technology zones to promote the growth of high technology startups headquartered there.[23] Even though it looks like merely a suggestion, in practice this stipulation has actually been used as an important indicator to assess the performance of local officials. In response to this mandatory 'suggestion', an array of venture capital funds or companies were established by local authorities in their own high technology zones between 1991 and 1997, most of them built with the support of the Torch Scheme. In this category, some have turned out to be a success while others have ended in failure or deviated from their initial missions. Next, two of the attempts will be picked out as samples to offer an overview of this historical stage.

Nanshan Venture Capital Fund[24]

With the incentive of the 'Provisional Regulation on the Policies of National High Technology Development Zones', the Nanshan District government of Shenzhen, a neighbor city to Hong Kong in southern China, planned to establish its own high technology zone with a specially appropriated fund worth RMB 2 billion. To complement this plan, the government of Nanshan District simultaneously begun the task of setting up and managing its own venture capital funds. In May of 1992, Nanshan Venture Capital Fund, with resources of RMB 109 million, was officially launched by the Nanshan District government. The first batch of investors into Nanshan Venture Capital Fund included China Southern Securities Company, which became insolvent in 2005, China Construction Bank Trust Investment Company, China Everbright Bank, China Village Development Trust Investment Company, which went bankrupt in 1998, China Ping An Insurance Company, and Shenzhen Nanshan District Investment Management Company. Half a year after its inception, Nanshan Venture Capital Fund was incorporated into a company called 'Shenzhen Nanshan Venture Capital Fund Company'.

Nanshan Venture Capital Fund was founded at the same time as the Chinese stock market and real estate market were beginning to bourgeon. At that time, many Chinese held an over-optimistic opinion that investing in stocks and real estate were the best ways to earn fast bucks. The management of Nanshan Venture Capital Fund did not escape from this mania. At the firm's outset, they laid down the investment guideline that Nanshan Venture Capital Fund ought to participate simultaneously in venture capital, stocks, and real estates. According to their explanation, the belief underlying this guideline was that Nanshan Venture Capital Fund would be able to make use of profits from investing in stocks and real estate to further support venture investment. Shortly afterwards, however, they discovered that not everything was to work out as they had initially anticipated.

Firstly, the management team of Nanshan Venture Capital Fund possessed little experience in screening business plans and then selecting out candidates which were promising. Consequently, they applied a vague and demanding set of criteria to searching for venture enterprises, such as high technology, high profits, and large markets. These criteria in turn gave rise to a dilemma: they felt that it was rather difficult to locate promising venture firms by adhering to these standards, and at the same time they felt that there were few venture firms which could satisfy them. As a result, they hesitated to fund entrepreneurs.

Secondly, the management team of Nanshan Venture Captial Fund lacked expertise in monitoring the operations of venture enterprises and providing them with valuable managerial advice. This lack of competence further exacerbated their hesitation and uncertainty in involving themselves in these 'troubles'. Incubating a venture firm generally demands huge financial injection. With only RMB 109 million in their hands, the entire management team thought that Nanshan Venture Capital Fund was yet to possess the ability to play the 'venture capital game'.

Thirdly, after investing in several high technology startups located in Shenzhen, the management of Nanshan Venture Capital Fund figured out that the waiting period for returns was much longer than they had previously anticipated. By contrast, Nanshan Venture Capital Fund reaped large, fast profits from stock and real estate investment. This difference further reduced the initial enthusiasm of the management of Nanshan Venture Capital Fund to develop its venture capital business.

The combination of the above three aspects made it impossible for Nanshan Venture Capital Fund to go far on the venture capital road. Statistics showed that venture capital investment accounted for less than 15 per cent of the annual investment of Nanshan Venture Capital Fund in 1993, with stock and real estate investment amounting to 57 per cent. On 26 January 1994, the management of Nanshan Venture Capital Fund decided that venture capital ought to be excluded from the investment portfolio of the fund. Since then, venture capital has been no more than a slogan of Nanshan Venture Capital Fund.

The case of Nanshan Venture Capital Fund represents the failed attempts of local governments to develop their own venture capital firms. Through the above description, it is clear that the failure of Nanshan Venture Capital Fund can be attributed principally to a lack of experience and a low level of risk tolerance among its management. It teaches us that the presence of experienced venture capitalists is essential for the prosperity of a country's venture capital market. It also implies that local attempts to develop venture capital can be successful if a professional management team is formed and relied upon. In this regard, Jiangsu Govtor Capital Company offers a good demonstration.

Jiangsu Govtor Capital Company[25]

Professor Ronald Gilson, a distinguished corporate law scholar at Stanford Law School, once wrote an article analyzing how a vibrant venture capital market can be engineered and what role government ought to play in this process. As he stated:

> At this level, developing a venture capital market confronts a difficult coordination problem that I will call simultaneity. A venture capital market requires the simultaneous availability of three factors, the provision of any one of which is contingent on the availability of the other two. A venture capital market requires (1) entrepreneurs,

(2) investors with the funds and the taste for high-risk, high-return investments, and (3) (as the discussion of U.S. venture capital contracting illustrates) a specialized financial intermediary to serve as the nexus of a set of sophisticated contracts. ... These three examples, together with the lessons of the U.S. venture capital contracting model, provide guidance in constructing a rough template for government efforts to engineer a venture capital market. The strategy reflects a central theme: The government should address the simultaneity problem by providing seed capital and helping to create the necessary financial intermediaries that together will encourage the supply of entrepreneurs, while at the same time maintaining the pattern of intense incentives coupled with intense monitoring that characterizes U.S. venture capital contracting.[26]

Through Professor Gilson's analysis, it becomes clear that a prosperous venture capital market is dependent on the simultaneous availability of large funds, specialized venture capital companies, and entrepreneurs. To address the simultaneity problem, what governments ought to do is to provide seed funds and help establish professional venture capital agencies which are immune from the intervention of any authorities. Next, the case of Jiangsu Govtor Capital Company will be introduced, the success of which is a demonstration of the above-mentioned model put forth by Professor Gilson.

Jiangsu Govtor Capital Company (Govtor Capital) was established by Jiangsu Provincial Government in July 1992. The mission of Govtor Capital was to manage and operate 'Jiangsu Technology Development Venture Fund' (Jiangsu Venture Fund), with an initial finance pool of RMB 0.3 billion. From Govtor Capital's inception, Jiangsu Provincial Government has made every effort to ensure Govtor Capital operates under a value-oriented model by inviting professionals to join its management team and avoiding undue administrative intervention into its operation. In order to further support the firm, Jiangsu Provincial Government decided to expand Jiangsu Venture Fund's resources to RMB 0.65 billion by the end of 2000. In addition, it also passed an ordinance entitled 'Provisional Administrative Methods of Jiangsu Technology Development Venture Fund' in June 2000, which refined the operational model of the fund. Pursuant to the ordinance, Jiangsu Venture Capital is under the management of Govtor Capital, which is obliged either to use part of the fund to set up new venture capital funds, with the capital operated by other venture capital agencies, or to directly commission other prestigious venture capital agencies to manage part of the fund. The mission of the fund is to support the growth of promising high technology startups. These actions taken by Jiangsu Provincial Government have guaranteed that sufficient and independent seed funds have already flooded into the hands of Govtor Capital. With regard to attracting venture capital professionals, Jiangsu Provincial Government invited Jinrong Xu and Wei Zhang respectively to take up the positions of chairman of the board of directors and CEO of Govtor Capital. Prior to joining Govtor Capital, Jinrong Xu, who is an expert in the venture capital market, worked for the Bureau of Public Finance of Jiangsu Province. Wei Zhang, who is a senior engineer, worked for the Bureau of Electronic Industry of Jiangsu Province. By teaming them up, Jiangsu Provincial Government has ensured that Jiangsu Venture Fund, under the management of Govtor Capital, can invest efficiently into selected high technology startups which possess the potential of high growth.

The efforts of Jiangsu Provincial Government have reaped swift rewards. In 2001, Govtor Capital invested in Suntech Company, at the time a small solar energy company. With five years' incubation by Govtor Capital, Suntech Company was successfully listed on the New York Stock Exchange at the end of 2005. Soon after that, Govtor Capital sold the Suntech stock it held on the secondary market, and harvested profits 238 times greater than its total investment in the company. The big success of its investment in Suntech did not slow down the pace of Govtor Capital and its management team. In 2007, Jinrong Xu and Wei Zhang decided to approve a capital injection into AMD Company, which focuses on developing and producing new materials. After more than four years of assistance from Govtor Capital, the IPO application of AMD Company was approved by the China Securities Regulatory Commission (CSRC) in September 2011. Through the listing of AMD Company on the Shenzhen Stock Exchange, Govtor Capital has made profits around 150 times greater than its investment into the company. So far, Govtor Capital has become one of the most successful domestic venture capital companies in China. In this sense, Jiangsu Provincial Government has also set an example for other local governments in China to follow when they aspire to build up their own venture capital sectors.

The third stage (1998-present)

1998 witnessed the initial proliferation of foreign venture capital and domestic privately-held firms in China. That year, the Central Committee of the Chinese National Democratic Constructive Association presented the 'Proposal for Developing China's Venture Capital Industry' at the 9th Chinese People's Political Consultative Conference.[27] The motion represented the end of the pilot phase of venture capital in China. As a result, the number of both foreign venture capital companies and Chinese privately-held firms, together with their respective investment funds, have increased rapidly. To vividly depict the features of this stage, two cases will be provided below. One relates to the successful operation of foreign venture capital in China, while the other displays the emergence of Chinese privately-held venture capital.

Focus Media[28]

At 8:30 a.m. on 13 July 2005, Nanchun Jiang, founder and chairman of the board of directors of Focus Media, stood in the front of the doorway of the NASDAQ and looked up at the giant plasma screen which was familiar to all entrepreneurs with the aspiration of floating their companies on the globally-renowned stock exchange. That day, Focus Media was officially listed on the NASDAQ, the birth of a media empire in China.

Back at college, Nanchun Jiang was director of the Summer Raindrop Student Poet Association of East China Normal University, located in Shanghai, and was subsequently elected chairman of the university's student union. Soon after his appointment, an advertising company affiliated with Shanghai Film Studio sought an intern from the members of the student union. Following the interview process, Nanchun Jiang ultimately acquired the offer. During his internship, the first task assigned to him was to draft an advertising proposal for a client with a budget of RMB 1500. He worked around the clock and quickly handed in his proposal to the client. To his surprise, the client was fairly satisfied with his idea and paid the advertising agency where he worked a generous amount of money to produce the advertisement. This first success inspired him to completely give up his duties in the student union and involve himself fully in the business of the advertising company.

In 1994, Nanchun Jiang, then a university junior aged 21, raised around RMB 1 million and founded his own advertising company named 'Yong Yi'. By the end of 1998, Yong Yi had claimed more than 95 per cent of the market share in IT-related advertisements in Shanghai, with an annual turnover between RMB 60 million and RMB 70 million. By 2001, its annual turnover reached RMB 150 million.

However, the continuing success of Yong Yi was halted by the bursting of IT bubbles worldwide in 2001. That year, its profits slumped drastically. In order to maintain the operation of his company, Nanjiang Chun had to explore advertising opportunities in small snack shops. Faced with hardship, Nanchun Jiang suddenly realized the vulnerability of the traditional advertising industry to the turbulence of the market. In turn, this realization finally pushed him to leave the niche with which he was familiar and take a new path.

On May 2002, Nanchun Jiang invested all his personal savings of RMB 20 million into equipping 50 top-tier office buildings in Shanghai with liquid crystal displays (LCDs), a brand new advertising model created by him. His innovation, however, was not immediately recognized by the market. Potential clients were hesitant to make use of the new platform to publicize themselves. Consequently, the initial fund of RMB 20 million quickly ran out. Nanjiang Chun and his company encountered a financial crisis.

At this critical moment, Nanchun Jiang made a decision to change his company's name from Yong Yi to Focus Media. Perhaps this change brought him good luck. Soon afterwards, Wei Yu, chief representative of SoftBank Shanghai Branch, approached Nanchun Jiang about the possibility of investing in Focus Media to help him develop his new advertising model. After several hours' negotiation, they concluded an investment agreement pursuant to which Focus Media would acquire an equity injection of $0.5 million from SoftBank. In the meanwhile, with the assistance of SoftBank, Focus Media also obtained another $0.5 million investment from another famous foreign venture capital agency named 'United Capital Investment Company'. This first round of fundraising of $1 million enabled Nanchun Jiang to fully lobby potential clients to accept his new advertising model, which turned out to be effective. More and more companies began to utilize the LCDs equipped by Focus Media in those office buildings in Shanghai to increase their exposure to the public. As a result, the business of Focus Media rapidly expanded across Shanghai and penetrated into another four Chinese cities. On March 2004, Nanchun Jiang and Focus Media secured the second round of syndicated fundraising from several prestigious foreign venture capital agencies, such as TDF, DFJ, and WI Harper Group. The newly raised $12.5 million further enlarged the business network of Focus Media and stabilized its leading role in the LCD advertisement industry. A mere nine months after the second round of fundraising, Focus Media concluded its third round of fundraising with $30 million from Goldman Sachs, 3i, and United Capital Investment Company. This round of capital inflow paved the way for Focus Media's subsequent listing on the NASDAQ. As the scenario at the beginning of this section described, Focus Media eventually opened on the stock exchange which had marked the glory and success of many big names. This great leap also earned those foreign venture capital agencies which participated in the building of the Focus Media empire huge monetary returns. Thus far, the success of Focus Media has become a microcosm of the sophisticated operation of foreign venture capital in China. To a large degree, the company has positioned itself at the top of the value chain of the Chinese venture capital market.

Fortune Capital[29]

In March 1999, for the first time, the CSRC explicitly put forward the suggestion that both Shanghai and Shenzhen stock exchanges might consider setting up high technology stock sectors on their main boards. Under such circumstances, Qiuyun Long, chairman of the board of directors of Hunan TV & Broadcast Intermediary Company (HTBIC), believed that the time for his company to join the venture capital market had come. Following a series of discussions with other senior members of the HTBIC, Qiuyun Long dispatched his assistant, Zhou Liu, to Shenzhen, with RMB 0.1 billion for the purpose of founding a venture capital company. On 19 April 2000, Shenzhen Fortune Capital Company (Fortune Capital) was officially incorporated and began its adventures in the venture capital market.

Soon after the incorporation of Fortune Capital, the IT bubble burst worldwide and, in turn, the global capital market underwent a downturn. Faced with these challenging market conditions, the newly-born Fortune Capital and its management team deeply tasted the perils of the financial industry. More seriously, dissenting voices arose in the HTBIC, which was the sole shareholder of Fortune Capital at that time. During this critical period, however, Qiuyun Long kept his nerve and continued to encourage Zhou Liu and his partners in Fortune Capital to persist with their venture.

The perseverance of Qiuyun Long was eventually rewarded in 2005. That year, the CRSC launched equity-division reform, which aimed to allow the shares of listed companies to be freely tradable on the secondary markets of Chinese stock exchanges. As a result, IPOs became an accessible means for venture capital firms to exit from their successful investee companies. One year after the reform, COSHIP Electronics Companies (COSHIP), one of the companies which made up Fortune Capital's venture capital portfolio, accomplished its IPO on the Shenzhen Stock Exchange. By exiting COSHIP at this time, Fortune Capital earned profits 30 times as great as its overall investment in the company. Subsequently, in July 2008, Talkweb Company, another member of Fortune Capital's investment portfolio, was also floated on the Shenzhen Stock Exchange, bringing Fortune Capital a 6000 per cent return. In 2009, the Growth Enterprise Market (GEM) was established as part of the Shenzhen Stock Exchange. During the following year, 10 members of Fortune Capital's portfolio were listed on the GEM, marking the establishment of its leading role among Chinese privately-held venture capital companies.

In an interview with Securities Times, which is an influential newspaper in China, Zhou Liu, chairman of the board of directors of Fortune Capital, ascribed the success of his company to the factors listed below.

Support from shareholders

As described above, the achievements of Fortune Capital are inseparable from the continuous support of the HTBIC that is the majority shareholder in the venture capital company. If the HTBIC had decided to dissolve Fortune Capital during the big recession of the IT industry in 2001, we would not have the chance to marvel at the miracle created by the venture capital agency.

Following foreign venture capital

Venture capital originated in Ancient Rome, and has prospered in America since the late 1970s. Therefore, foreign venture capital companies, especially American ones, have already accumulated sophisticated experience in this market. For Fortune Capital, as a newcomer in this field, it was necessary to first learn the successful operation of foreign venture capital as it developed its own market and constructed its own reputation.

Prudent investment

The venture capital market offers high risks as well as high profits. Thus, with the intention of increasing the success rate of its investments, Fortune Capital has made every effort to scrutinize each investment for prudence. It is the company's belief that success is always closely associated with risk control ex ante.

An outstanding business plan

The first stage of prudential investment is to select outstanding business plans. At Fortune Capital, two standards have been adopted to judge the quality of business proposals. The first benchmark focuses on the marketability of the products described by business proposals. The second is concerned with the budget necessary to produce the products. Only a product featuring both high marketability and low costs is deemed worthy of investment.

Good timing

Even if a good business plan has been spotted, investment also needs to be well-timed. As far as Fortune Capital is concerned, good timing is usually the period when a certain industry is suffering from recession. For example, the Chinese livestock feeding industry was badly hit by avian flu in 2006. Fortune Capital seized this opportunity to make an equity investment into a chicken feeding company at a discounted price. Three years later, the same company successfully opened on the stock exchange, making Fortune Capital huge profits.

Qualified project managers

Qualified project managers are extremely important to venture capital companies, Fortune Capital pays close attention to this aspect of its operations. It has designed various training programs to acquaint its project managers with the latest listing policies, business models, accounting, and legal rules. In addition, the company emphasizes the necessity of project managers forming good habits, such as self-discipline and self-motivation.

Incentives

Rational people always respond to incentives, a fact which is fully understood by Fortune Capital. To constrain the opportunistic behaviors of project managers and incentivize them into working as hard as possible, Fortune Capital has devised an incentive system. For example, 2–3 per cent of the profits accruing from a project are used to reward the project managers who participate in the project from beginning to end. In addition, Fortune Capital has also granted key members a portion of stocks to motivate and stabilize them. Decisions about promotion are based entirely on performance. In other words, positions at each level of Fortune Capital are always open to the best performers.

A current profile of the Chinese venture capital market

The second part of this book has sketched out the historical development of the Chinese venture capital market. Broadly speaking, the concept of 'venture capital' burgeoned in China in the early 1980s. Until 1998, however, the development of venture capital was dominated by the efforts of both the Chinese Central Government and local governments. In 1998, the Central Committee of the Chinese National Democratic Constructive Association presented the 'Proposal for Developing China's Venture Capital Industry' at the Ninth Chinese People's Political Consultative Conference. Since then, venture capital has become a fast growing segment of China's financial system.[30] During the last 14 years, China has made remarkable progress in the development of its venture capital market. Table 1.1 shows the total amounts of venture capital under management in China every year between 2003 and 2006. By looking at Table 1.1, the conclusion can be easily drawn that the total amount of venture capital under management in China is trending upwards. By 2006, the amount had increased almost twofold in comparison with 2003.

Table 1.2 reflects the amount of venture capital invested annually in China from 2003 to 2006. The trend in annual venture capital investment is also upward: the amount in 2006 was nearly four times as much as in 2003.

The striking expansion of China's venture capital market, however, cannot disguise the embarrassing fact that Chinese domestic venture capital has been marginalized by foreign investment. In other words, foreign venture capital is playing a leading role in China's venture capital market. Table 1.3 displays the differences in annual investment from Chinese domestic venture capital and foreign venture capital in China between 2005 and 2007. It is clear that the percentage of annual investment made by Chinese domestic venture capital is shrinking. As Table 1.3 shows, this number decreased sharply from 43.1 per cent in 2005 to 24 per cent in 2007.

Table 1.1 **Total amount of venture capital under management in China between 2003 and 2006**

Year	2003	2004	2005	2006
Amount (Billion RMB)	32.534	43.87	46.45	58.385

Source: China Venture Capital Yearbook (2007).[31]

Table 1.2 **Annual amounts of venture capital investment in China between 2003 and 2006**

Year	2003	2004	2005	2006
Amount (Billion RMB)	3.715	3.783	11.757	14.364

Source: China Venture Capital Yearbook (2007).[32]

Table 1.3 **Differences in annual investment between domestic VCs and foreign VCs in China, 2005 to 2007**

Investment size		Domestic venture capital	Foreign venture capital	Total
2007	Number of Projects	412	329	741
	Percentage of Projects	55.6%	44.4%	100%
	Investment Amount (Billion RMB)	9.554	30.250	39.804
	Percentage of Investment	24%	76%	100%
Average Investment Amount in 2007 (Thousand RMB)		23,885.6	12,2470.4	61,521.5
2006	Number of Projects	219	152	371
	Percentage of Projects	59.03%	40.97%	100%
	Investment Amount (Billion RMB)	3.43	10.93	14.36
	Percentage of Investment	23.91%	76.09%	100%
Average Investment Amount in 2006 (Thousand RMB)		16,432.6	79,774.6	41,513.1
2005	Number of Projects	215	143	358
	Percentage of Projects	60.1%	39.9%	100%
	Investment Amount (Billion RMB)	2.358	3.110	5.468
	Percentage of Investment	43.1%	56.9%	100%

Source: China Venture Capital Yearbook (2007–2008).[33]

Table 1.4 exhibits the differences in total registered capital between Chinese domestic venture capital institutions and foreign venture capital institutions in China from 2005 to 2007. In this regard, consonant with Table 1.3, foreign venture capital also holds an overwhelming advantage over its domestic rivals in China.

Table 1.4 **Differences in total registered capital between domestic VC institutions and foreign VC institutions in China, 2005 to 2007**

Type	Domestic venture capital	Foreign venture capital	Total
Amount in 2007 (Billion RMB)	22.335	44.078	66.413
Percentage in 2007	33.63%	66.37%	100%
Mean Value in 2007 (Thousand RMB)	65,000	98,125	66,000
Amount in 2006 (Billion RMB)	14.951	45.874	60.825
Percentage in 2006	24.58%	75.42%	100%
Mean Value in 2006 (Thousand RMB)	65,000	88,125	66,000
Percentage in 2005	35%	65%	100%

Source: China Venture Capital Yearbook (2007–2008).[34]

The above data depicts the contours of the Chinese venture capital market during a time that Chinese domestic venture capital has been marginalized by its foreign competitors. Objectively speaking, the current disadvantageous situation plaguing Chinese domestic venture capital is a result of multiple factors. As stated in the introduction, however, this book concentrates on the negative role played by the legal system in the weak competitive ability of Chinese domestic venture capital in comparison with its foreign rivals. In other words, Chinese venture capital legislation will be analyzed to determine which components of it have created impediments to the healthy development of Chinese domestic venture capital. In order to highlight the defects of Chinese venture capital jurisprudence, the institutional ecology that has nurtured the prosperity of the American venture capital market will be used for comparison. This model has been empirically proven to be duplicable by different countries, and is currently followed by most foreign venture capital firms, included but not limited to American ones.

With regard to the institutional environment that has created an active venture capital market in America, western legal and financial scholars have already held thorough discussions. On the basis of their contributions, three key traits of the institutional structure for the success of the American venture capital market have been isolated: the availability of large and independent funding, the application of organizational and contractual incentive mechanisms, and the existence of efficient exit channels. These three key traits also constitute the whole cycle of venture capital.

According to the above analysis, the remaining parts of this book will proceed as follows. Chapter 2 will explore fundraising for Chinese venture capital. In this regard, American venture capital tells us that institutional investors play an indispensable role. Based on American wisdom regarding the fundraising of venture capital, relevant laws and regulations in China will be examined in this chapter to determine whether they have prevented Chinese institutional investors, including pension funds, commercial banks, and insurance companies, from co-operating actively with Chinese domestic venture capital. Chapter 3 will discuss the application of organizational and contractual incentive mechanisms in Chinese domestic venture capital. Firstly, the organizational structure of limited partnership, which is usually adopted by American venture funds, was absent for a long time in China. Although the revised Partnership Enterprise Law has encouraged this form of organization, the number of limited partnerships has remained small, which has limited the effectiveness of this change. Secondly, staged financing and board representation are commonly applied by Chinese domestic venture capital. In most cases, however, their real functions have been significantly distorted and weakened. Thirdly, stock options as an incentive device offered to venture-capital-backed entrepreneurs in America are undeveloped in Chinese domestic venture capital. Fourthly, convertible preferred stocks, a kind of protective tool for American venture capital, were prohibited from use by Chinese domestic venture capital for a long time. Although this has been liberalized since 2005, the lack of a regulation which specifies their issuance procedure has hindered their full application by, and efficacy for, Chinese domestic venture capital. Chapter 4 will examine the exit of Chinese domestic venture capital through the Chinese domestic stock market. First, the listing requirements of the main boards of the Shanghai Stock Exchange and the Shenzhen Stock Exchange are too high to be achieved by enterprises backed by Chinese domestic venture capital. Likewise, the Small and Medium-sized Enterprises Board of the Shenzhen Stock Exchange (SME Board) has also adopted high listing standards, making this route less workable and attractive for Chinese domestic venture capital. Moreover, the Growth Enterprise Market (GEM) was absent from China's stock market for a long period. Although it was opened in 2009, it has placed too much emphasis on financing and, to a large degree, ignored the authentic exits of Chinese domestic venture capital. Additionally, the forbidden liquidity of state-owned shares and legal person shares on the Chinese stock market, before the equity division reform and bureaucratic listing approval procedures, have also handicapped the prompt and smooth exits of Chinese domestic venture capital from their portfolio companies. The final chapter will predict how long it will take to weed out the legal barriers existing in the whole cycle of Chinese domestic venture capital.

Fundraising for Chinese venture capital: legal problems and reform measures

2

A profile of fundraising for American venture capital

The nature of venture capital, and its provision of capital for high-risk, high potential startup companies, determines that it is a financial sector featuring huge investments in projects.[35] Generally speaking, a venture capitalist needs to infuse capital into a portfolio company during several rounds of funding to incubate the potentially profitable technology invented by the company through the growth period and eventually market it to consumers in the form of mature products.[36] The total infusion of capital usually adds up to millions of dollars. Therefore, not only does the venture capital industry mean high risks and high rewards, but it also requires large funds.

An obvious reason for the vitality of the American venture capital market is that venture capitalists are able to obtain a sufficient influx of finance, which enables them to satisfy the substantial pecuniary needs of their portfolio companies.[37] If we look back at the history of the American venture capital industry, however, we realize that its origin was not accompanied by massive monetary injection. As mentioned earlier, the first genuine venture capital organization in America was American Research and Development (ARD), set up in 1946 by former MIT President Karl Compton, General Georges F. Doriot, who was a professor at Harvard Business School, and some local commercial leaders.[38] During its 26-year existence, ARD raised funds principally from individuals and seldom required the involvement of institutional investors due to regulatory barriers.[39] This lack of capital led to ARD investing primarily in comparatively small entities. For example, it invested only 70,000 US dollars in Digital Equipment Corporation, which generated almost half of ARD's overall profits during its lifespan.[40] At that time, the fundraising dilemma faced by ARD was not exceptional and was a microcosm of the American venture capital industry at its early stage.

The dramatic growth of investment in the American venture capital industry occurred in the late 1970s.[41] With regard to the forces that generated these striking movements in venture capital fundraising, American economic and legal scholars have conducted full discussions in their publications.[42] Among all the factors which they have identified, the Department of Labor's clarification of the 'prudent man' rule in 1979 has played the most significant role in practice.[43] Prior to that amendment, the Employee Retirement Income Security Act (ERISA) forbade pension funds to invest substantial amounts of money in VC or other high-risk financial instruments.[44] The Department of Labor's explication of the rule permitted pension fund managers to invest freely in high-risk assets, including venture capital. This change of regulatory requirement opened the floodgates to the utilization of the tremendous capital resources held in pension resources, and contributed considerably to the increase of money flowing into the venture capital sector.[45] Table 2.1 shows that pension funds became the single largest source of capital for American venture capital, and accounted for almost half of all contributions after 1978. Therefore, it is fair to say that pension funds have played the most salient part in the development of the sizable fundraising for the American venture capital market. This is also why the capital volume of the venture capital industry in America has remained high during the past 20 years, even though it has been through several ebbs.[46]

Beyond the amount of funding, the relationship between venture capitalists and their principal investors is also critical to the vitality of a venture capital market.[48] As Curtis Milhaupt pointed out, 'venture capitalists can be expected to behave differently – to have different investment and exit strategies and performance expectations – depending on their relationship with their principal investors'.[49] When operating independently of major venture investors, the venture capitalist is allowed to focus on nurturing the most promising ventures and reaping the harvests of those investments. In turn, this successful experience encourages subsequent capital injection from investors. If, in contrast, the venture capitalist is affected substantially by the intentions of major investors, it's likely that he will perform in a way which is divergent from the mission of maximizing the profits of investment.[50] Consequently, this will negatively influence capital contribution both from the supply side and demand side.

In America, pension funds as the single largest source of capital have guaranteed the independent status of venture capitalists. Pension fund managers invest in venture capital funds in order to seek returns and enhance diversification.[51] Therefore, as per the pertinent analysis made by Curtis Milhaupt, 'the pension manager's investment decision reflects the calculation about the skill of the venture capitalist in ferreting out opportunities that promise a high rate of return'.[52] The importance of the independence of venture capitalists is also evidenced by the failure of the Japanese venture capital industry, whose venture capitalists are generally affiliated with the principal investors – large banks and securities firms.[53]

As for the capital of American venture capital agencies which operate in China, the overwhelming majority of it is raised within the territory of America. On the one hand, this fact has ensured that these American venture capital companies possess adequate money throughout the whole process of investment.[54] On the other hand, it also implicitly reflects the difficulties in pooling RMB funds faced by foreign venture capital. Although the Chinese authorities have approved several of them to directly or indirectly establish RMB funds, foreign venture capital is still very cautious and passive about exercising this option, taking into account the high costs of doing business in China – the time-consuming approval procedure, the underdevelopment of limited partnerships, the limited sources of finance, and the uncertainty of liquidity through Chinese stock markets.[55] Therefore, American venture capitalists are more likely to rely on their compatriot venture capital investors than on Chinese ones.

The above success story of fundraising in the American venture capital industry presents us with two valuable points from both the theoretical and practical viewpoints. Firstly, pension funds can make great contributions to the capital growth of

Table 2.1 Summary of statistics for venture capital fundraising in America, 1978 to 2002

Year	Number of funds	Size ($ mil)	Pension funds (%)	Corporations (%)	Individuals (%)	Endowments (%)	Insurance companies and banks (%)	Foreign investors and others (%)
1978	23	495	15	10	32	9	16	18
1979	27	560	31	17	23	10	4	15
1980	57	1,444	30	19	16	14	13	8
1981	81	1,984	23	17	23	12	15	10
1982	98	2,420	33	12	21	7	14	13
1983	147	6,319	31	12	21	8	12	16
1984	150	5,608	34	14	15	6	13	18
1985	99	4,856	33	12	13	8	11	23
1986	86	51	51	11	12	6	10	11
1987	112	6,232	39	10	12	10	15	14
1988	78	4,309	47	12	8	11	9	13
1989	88	4,007	36	20	6	12	13	13
1990	50	2,905	53	7	11	13	9	7
1991	34	1,771	42	4	12	24	6	12
1992	31	2,331	42	3	11	18	14	11
1993	54	2,949	59	8	7	11	11	4
1994	105	5,524	47	9	12	21	9	2
1995	72	5,283	38	2	17	22	18	3
1996	97	9,185	43	13	9	21	5	8
1997	136	12,676	40	30	13	9	1	7
1998	281	32,904	60	12	11	6	10	N/A
1999	421	62,053	43	14	10	17	16	N/A
2000	614	108,382	40	4	12	21	23	N/A
2001	299	40,648	42	3	9	22	25	N/A
2002	125	8,005	45	10	12	11	16	6

Source: The Venture Capital Cycle.[47]

a venture capital market. If pension funds are not available, there must be alternative institutional investors of similar size and nature to take their place. Secondly, the independent status of venture capitalists plays a critical role in the presence of a vibrant venture capital industry. The combination of these two aspects is partly responsible for the outstanding character of American venture capital – the high risk tolerance demonstrated by the preference for frontier high technologies and early-stage investment.[56]

Chinese pension funds

In the early 1950s, the newly-born socialist regime faced numerous tricky problems. Among them, two related to the welfare of workers in industrial enterprises. Firstly, based on Marxism and Leninism, the group of workers in industrial enterprises was defined as 'the leading class of the People's Republic of China'. Then, a question naturally arose regarding how the welfare of the leading class could be achieved and secured. Secondly, at that time, the primary economic mission of the new regime was quickly to accomplish industrialization as the former Soviet Union had already done. It was the understanding of the supreme leaders of the CPC that the accomplishment of industrialization was dependent upon the enthusiasm of workers in industrial factories. In turn, one solution to this problem was to devise a welfare system to incentivize workers to contribute as much of their strength as possible to quickly realizing industrialization in China.[57]

Given that it was the most important part of the whole system, the Chinese Central Government began engineering the welfare system for industrial workers by first setting up pension funds. On 26 February 1955, it enacted a regulation entitled 'Provisional Regulation on Labor Insurance'.[58] Pursuant to this regulation, pension funds of industrial workers were fully assumed by the enterprises where the workers were affiliated. In other words, once a person became an industrial worker, his enterprise was obligated to pay him salaries until he passed away.[59] Apart from pension funds, industrial enterprises were also responsible for providing free medical care, free housing, and other benefits to their employees. This welfare model is known as 'enterprises running the whole society'.[60] Objectively speaking, this mode was compatible with the then-dominant centrally-planned economy, because enterprises were only the units to implement the directives of governments and were not concerned with their own profits and losses during that period. This approach also pushed the industrialization process of China to some degree, through the use of economic incentives to arouse the enthusiasm of workers.

In 1966, Zedong Mao, Chairman of the CPC, launched the devastating Cultural Revolution to purge Shaoqi Liu, Xiaoping Deng, and their allies. During the 10-year disaster stemming from this power struggle, ordinary Chinese people become feverish in their determination to demonstrate their loyalty to Chairman Mao. In accordance with the commands of Chairman Mao, workers in industrial enterprises no longer performed their duties in production, and instead involved themselves in a political farce to protect Chairman Mao from being ousted by his opponents. Consequently, almost all the enterprises in China found it impossible to maintain normal operation during this ridiculous age.[61] The paralysis of industrial enterprises in turn negatively influenced the established welfare system, which subsumed pension funds. Even though the retirement system was still in place, the monthly salary of retired workers was hardly increased during the Cultural Revolution, partly due to the financial crisis caused by the quasi-suspension of industrial production nationwide. In this sense, the operation of pension funds was in stagnation from 1966 to 1976.[62]

1978 marked the end of the Cultural Revolution. Xiaoping Deng, who was purged by Zedong Mao during the 10-year political movement, returned to claim power. With his advocacy, China has been going through a far-reaching transformation from a centrally-planned economy to a market-oriented one. Concomitant with the establishment of the market economy, numerous small and medium-sized SOEs have been divested by governments and become privately-held entities. These controlled transactions created a new problem regarding the establishment of pension funds for employees working in privately-held enterprises: the existing scheme only covered the workers in SOEs, which were pervasive in the age of the centrally-planned economy. Confronted with this difficulty, the Chinese Central Government began to overhaul the Maoist pension scheme. After a series of attempts, it released a regulation entitled 'Decision of the State Council to Reform the Pension Scheme of SOEs' (1991 Decision) in 1991. The result of this was that the pensions of SOE workers were no longer assumed exclusively by enterprises, but were shared proportionally by workers and enterprises.[63] In other words, SOE workers had to take out a small portion of their monthly salaries to contribute to their future pensions. This change reduced the financial burden of SOEs to some degree. More importantly, it also paved the way for the implementation of pension schemes in emerging privately-held enterprises. In 1995, on the basis of the 1991 Decision, the Chinese Central Government released a circular named 'Notice regarding the Further Reform of the Pension Scheme in Enterprises'.[64] This circular had twofold significance. Firstly, it announced the birth of the quasi-governmental pension institution which is in charge of the money pool created by the enterprise pension scheme. Secondly, it marked the extension of the enterprise pension scheme from SOEs into both privately-held and foreign-invested enterprises. At the time of writing, this pattern of pension scheme is still valid for all types of enterprises in China.[65]

Apart from the employees of enterprises, the majority of Chinese populations live in villages. Differing from enterprise workers, who are affiliated with their employer units, Chinese farmers dwell loosely in their villages, which are defined as non-profit autonomous organizations by the Chinese Constitution. Consequently, villages are financially unable to pay pensions to their farmers as enterprises do for their workers. Hence, the question of how to fill the gap in pensions for Chinese farmers was a tricky problem facing the Chinese Central Government back in the early 1990s.[66]

In 1992, the Ministry of Civil Affairs of the PRC enacted a regulation entitled 'Basic Scheme of Pension Funds for Farmers (Provisional)', which marked the appearance of pension funds in vast numbers of Chinese villages.[67] According to the scheme, farmers who were willing to subscribe to the scheme were required first to open their own pension accounts at the agency in-charge of their local governments. After that, they could choose to pay a monthly premium ranging from RMB 2 to RMB

12, at their discretion, for several years. These premiums would accumulate in their pension accounts at the yearly interest rate of 7.5 per cent. Then, they were eligible to claim a pension payment from their local governments on a monthly basis from the age of 60 onwards.[68] Soon after the release of the scheme, hundreds of thousands of farmers took out money from their pockets to join it, in the hope that they would live a stable elder life with sustainable pensions from their governments. Over the next decade, however, the situation became embarrassing for the local governments, owing to a fundamental defect of the seemingly well-conceived scheme, as described below.

Back in 1992, when the scheme was launched, the yearly deposit interest rate of Chinese state-owned commercial banks was around 10.8 per cent, and the average monthly salary of a worker in an SOE was about RMB 200. Based mainly on these two parameters, the Ministry of Civil Affairs of the PRC set the yearly interest rate of the farmer pension scheme at 7.5 per cent, confident that the yearly deposit interest rate of state-owned commercial banks would never be lower than 7.5 per cent, and hence governments would never default on their obligation to pay pensions to farmers subscribing to the scheme as long as they deposited premiums into state-owned commercial banks. In addition, with a yearly interest rate of 7.5 per cent and a monthly minimum premium of RMB 2, a farmer could receive a monthly pension payment of RMB 50–60, with which he would live a good life in his village given average consumption levels in China in the early 1990s. The subsequent rapid development of China's economy, however, heavily battered the simplistic and unrealistic predictions inherent in the scheme. Firstly, facing a badly insufficient domestic consumption demand, the People's Bank of China, the Chinese central bank, has continuously lowered the deposit interest rate of state-owned commercial banks to boost the consumption of ordinary people since the middle of the 1990s. As a result, the deposit interest rate of state-owned commercial banks has quickly fallen below 7.5 per cent, fatally paralyzing the operation of the farmer pension scheme. Secondly, the income level of Chinese citizens has risen substantially since 1997. Consequently, with a monthly payment of RMB 50–60, even a farmer in the most remote village in China could not sustain his life. The combination of these two upheavals signaled the failure of the farmer pension scheme.[69] In 1999, the State Council officially suspended its operations on the ground on the grounds that it was not ready to offer a pension scheme to Chinese farmers. This suspension led to a vacuum of pensions in Chinese villages for 10 years. In 2009, however, the State Council re-launched a new pension scheme, featuring a combination of fiscal subsidy and personal subscription, to thousands of millions of Chinese farmers. Thus far, the result of this new attempt is still unknown to all of us.[70]

Currently, Chinese pension funds, together with unemployment insurance, work-related injury insurance, medical insurance, and maternity insurance, are officially called 'social security funds', which are in the charge of the National Council for Social Security Fund (SSF).[71] Generally speaking, the SSF tends to put up social security funds as a whole for investment purposes rather than using an individual funding source. As Table 2.2 illustrates, pension funds account for the overwhelming majority of the total volume of social security funds. Therefore, 'Social security fund' will be considered the equivalent of 'pension funds' in the Chinese context in this book.

Table 2.2 Social security funds in China

Year	Total (RMB 100 mil)	Pension funds	Unemployment insurance	Medical insurance	Work injury insurance	Maternity insurance
1990	186.8	178.8	8.0	N/A	N/A	N/A
1991	225	215.7	9.3	N/A	N/A	N/A
1992	377.4	365.8	11.7	N/A	N/A	N/A
1993	526.1	503.5	17.9	1.4	2.4	0.8
1994	742	707.4	25.4	3.2	4.6	1.5
1995	1,006	950.1	35.3	9.7	8.1	2.9
2000	2,644.5	2,278.1	160.4	170.0	24.8	11.2
2001	3,101.9	2,489.0	187.3	383.6	28.3	13.7
2002	4,048.7	3,171.5	215.6	607.8	32.0	21.8
2003	4,882.9	3,680.0	249.5	890.0	37.6	25.8
2004	5,780.3	4,258.4	291.0	1140.5	58.3	32.1

Source: China Labor Statistical Yearbook (2005).[72]

The current statute regulating the investment of social security funds in China is the 'Provisional Regulation of National Social Security Funds' Investment', promulgated jointly by the MOF and the Ministry of Labor and Social Security in 2001. Article 28 of this regulation explicitly stipulates the financial instruments in which social security funds are permitted to invest and their respective receivable investment amounts. Article 28 stipulates that the investment of social security funds in the form of bank deposits and national debts be not less than 50 per cent of their overall volume; that investment of social security funds in the form of enterprise bonds and financial bonds be not more than 10 per cent of their overall volume; that investment of social security funds in the form of mutual funds and stocks be not more than 40 per cent of their overall volume.[73] Apparently, venture capital is excluded from the investment categories of social security funds permitted by Article 28.

Chinese commercial banks

Soon after the inception of the People's Republic of China in 1949, the CPC launched a movement to nationalize privately-held enterprises. By the end of 1956, this movement led to the establishment of a state-owned economy in China, which was distinguished by the pervasiveness of SOEs. In addition, consistent with the dominance of the state-owned economy, the CPC also replicated the centrally-planned system of the former Soviet Union to manage production and allocate resources in the county. With regard to commercial banking, the supremacy of the centrally-planned system was illustrated by the fact that the People's Bank of China became the only commercial bank in mainland China at that time, through converting all the other commercial banks to the ranks of its internal divisions. In other words, before the implementation of the policy of reform and opening-up in the late 1970s, the People's Bank of China monopolized the business of taking deposits, making loans, and exchanging foreign currency in socialist China. Meanwhile, apart from exercising the function of sole commercial bank, the People's Bank of China was simultaneously authorized to act as the Chinese central bank by the State Council. As a result, it was both an 'athlete' and a 'referee' in the Chinese commercial bank sector until the early 1980s. More harmfully, from September 1969 to March 1978, the People's Bank of China lost its independence and became an agency subordinated to the MOF. This led to it handling both fiscal revenues and personal deposits and fundamentally disobeyed the rationale underlying the operation of commercial banks.[74]

Following the end of the Cultural Revolution in 1976, the CPC, led by Mr. Xiaoping Deng, embarked on rectifying the errors made in the past 10 years of catastrophe. Independence was restored to the People's Bank of China by the MOF in March 1978, but it still maintained its dual status as a commercial bank and the Chinese central bank. In February 1979, the State Council decided to detach the Agricultural Bank of China from the People's Bank of China and turn it into an independent commercial bank, mainly providing financial services to villages and farmers. Subsequently, the State Council liberated another two commercial banks, the Bank of China and the Construction Bank of China respectively, from the People's Bank of China in March

1979 and from the MOF in August 1979. The Bank of China has been authorized to offer financial services related to exports and foreign currency, while the Construction Bank of China has been designated to be responsible for long-term loans. In September 1983, the State Council made the decision to take the business of commercial banking away from the People's Bank of China, and have it function only as the central bank. Meanwhile, the business of commercial banking was transferred to a newly-established commercial bank named the 'Industrial and Commercial Bank of China', which symbolized the dominance of the four state-owned commercial banks in the post-1970s Chinese commercial banking sector.[75] Since then, although dozens of joint-stock commercial banks and local commercial banks have been incorporated in the following 30 years, the Big Four system has not been fundamentally shaken.[76] Next, brief introductions will be made to the four biggest commercial banks in China.

Bank of China[77]

The history of the Bank of China dates back to the year 1905, when the dying Qing Dynasty issued an edict to establish the Daqing Hubu Bank in Beijing. Three years later, the Daqing Hubu Bank was renamed the Daqing Bank. In 1912, the Qing Dynasty was eventually toppled by an uprising led by the Kuomintang (KMT), and the Republic of China was founded in the same year. Soon after its inception, the new republic renamed the Daqing Bank the Bank of China and further authorized it to play the role of central bank.

In 1949, the KMT as well as the Republic of China, under its rule, lost a civil war against the CPC and retreated to Taiwan. There, the Bank of China was restructured and continued to offer financial services until 1971, when it was privatized and transformed into the International Commercial Bank of China, which has subsequently merged with the Taiwan Bank of Communications to become the Mega International Commercial Bank.

The operation of the Bank of China has also been maintained by the CPC since the withdrawal of the KMT to Taiwan in 1949. For quite a long time, however, it existed only as an internal agency of the People's Bank of China. In 1979, the State Council of the PRC decided to detach it from the People's Bank of China and make it operate as an independent commercial bank. In 2009, in terms of existing statistics, it was the 2nd largest lender in mainland China overall, and the 5th largest bank in the world by market capitalization value. It was once wholly owned by the Chinese Central Government, via Central Huijin Investment Ltd. and the SSF. In 2006, it finalized its IPOs respectively on the Hong Kong Stock Exchange and the Shanghai Stock Exchange. In the Forbes Global 2000, a list of the world's largest companies, it ranked 21st in 2012. By the end of 2011, its total assets had reached RMB 11,830 billion and the deposit pool under its management amounted to RMB 7,282.091 billion.

The Bank of China is regarded as the most international Chinese commercial bank, with outlets on every continent. Outside of mainland China, 'it also operates in 27 countries including Australia, Canada, United Kingdom, Ireland, France, Germany, Italy, Luxembourg, Russia, Hungary, United States, Panama, Brazil, Japan, the Republic of Korea, Singapore, Taiwan, Philippines, Vietnam, Malaysia, Thailand,

Indonesia, Kazakhstan, Bahrain, Zambia, South Africa, and a branch office in the Cayman Islands. In December 2010, its New York branch began offering RMB products for Americans. It was the first major Chinese bank to offer such a product.' In addition, it is also licensed to issue banknotes in China's two special administrative regions, Hong Kong and Macau, along with other commercial banks there, though it is not the Chinese central bank. It is fair to say that, as the oldest commercial bank in China, the Bank of China has witnessed the birth, development, transformation, and reform of the Chinese banking industry over the past century.

The agricultural bank of China[78]

Following the foundation of the PRC in 1949, the Agricultural Bank of China went through a series of changes. Originally, it consisted of the Farmers Bank of China and the Co-operation Bank, which were established and managed by the Republic of China before it retreated to Taiwan in 1949. These were merged to form the Agricultural Co-operation Bank in 1951, based on the instructions of the Central Government of the PRC. The Agricultural Co-operation Bank is regarded as the predecessor of the Agricultural Bank of China. However, only one year after its incorporation, the bank was merged into the People's Bank of China and became one of its internal agencies. Three years after the merger, another bank with the name of 'the Agricultural Bank of China' was established by the Chinese Central Government. Then, it too was merged into the People's Bank of China in 1957. Interestingly, the Chinese Central Government played the game again in 1963, by incorporating a new bank with the name of 'the Agricultural Bank of China'. Once again, this new Agricultural Bank of China was merged into the People's Bank of China two years after its inception. The current Agricultural Bank of China was detached from the People's Bank of China in February 1979.

Nowadays, the Agricultural Bank of China has become one of the leading commercial banks in China. It is principally committed to satisfying the financial needs of Chinese villages, farmers, and the Chinese agricultural industry. In addition, it has also striven to move into the international financial market by providing diversified financial services to foreign clients. According to its official website, it does this by 'capitalizing on the comprehensive business portfolio, extensive distribution network and advanced IT platform, it provides various corporate and retail banking products and services for a broad range of customers and carries out treasury operations for its own accounts or on behalf of customers covering investment banking, fund management, financial leasing and so on. At the end of 2011, it had total assets of RMB 11,677.577 billion, deposits of RMB 9,622.026 billion and loans of RMB 5,628.705 billion. Its capital adequacy ratio and non-performing loan ratio were 11.94 per cent and 1.55 per cent, respectively. It achieved a net profit of RMB 121.956 billion.' At the time of writing, it has opened overseas branches or representative offices in Singapore, Hong Kong, Seoul, New York, Dubai, Tokyo, Frankfurt, Sydney, Vancouver, and Hanoi.

The Agricultural Bank of China was successfully listed on both the Hong Kong Stock Exchange and the Shanghai Stock Exchange in July 2010, which was the world's biggest ever IPO. According to statistics in 2011, 'it ranked 127th in the Fortune Global 500 and ranked 7th in the Banker's Top 1000 World Banks list in terms of profits before taxation in the year of 2010. In 2011, its long term deposits rating/ outlook was assigned A1/Stable by Moody's Investors Service and its long term credit rating/bank stability and outlook were assigned A/B+ and Stable by Fitch Ratings.'

China construction bank[79]

The history of the China Construction Bank can be traced back to 1954, when it was established under the name of the People's Construction Bank of China, as an integral affiliate of the MOF, to manage the pool of funds for the construction of the new country. This status lasted until 1979, when the State Council decided to liberate it from the MOF and task it with more commercial bank responsibilities. Since then, the People's Construction Bank of China functioned as both a policy-oriented bank and a commercial one until 1994.

In 1994, the State Council decided to divest the business of the policy-oriented bank from the People's Construction Bank of China and transferred it to a newly-established policy-oriented bank named 'China Development Bank'. Since then, it has become a genuine leading commercial bank in China. In 1996, its name was changed to China Construction Bank.

On 14 September 2004, the China Banking Regulatory Commission approved the application of the China Construction Bank to split into the China Construction Bank Corporation, which functions as a commercial bank, and China Jianyin Investment Ltd, which functions as an investment bank. On 17 September 2004, the China Construction Bank Corporation was officially incorporated in the organizational form of a joint stock company, as provided for by the Chinese Company Law of the time. On 27 October 2005, the China Construction Bank Corporation was listed on the Hong Kong Stock Exchange. On 25 September 2007, it was also listed on the Shanghai Stock Exchange. According to statistics, its total assets reached RMB 8.7 trillion in 2009. In 2011, it ranked 2nd among all commercial banks in the world by market capitalization and was the 13th largest company in the world.

Between 2002 and 2005, however, the China Construction Bank Corporation was drawn into the mire of scandals. As described by Wiki, 'in January 2002, its Chairman Xuebing Wang resigned from the bank after being charged with accepting bribes while he was employed by the Bank of China; he was sentenced to 12 years in prison. In March 2005, his successor, Enzhao Zhang, resigned for 'personal reasons'. Just prior to his resignation, he had been charged in a lawsuit with accepting a $1 million bribe. He was later sentenced to 15 years in jail in connection with the case.'

These scandals never hampered the steps taken by the China Construction Bank toward becoming a first-class international commercial bank. 'In 2006, it acquired the Bank of America (Asia), which started in 1912 in Hong Kong as the Bank of Canton, and had a subsidiary in Macao. In 2008, it submitted an application to the New York State Banking Department and the Federal Reserve Board to establish a branch in New York City. It officially opened its New York branch on 6 June 2009.' Four days before the opening of the New York branch, it launched its London office. So far, it has maintained overseas branches in Frankfurt, Hong Kong, Johannesburg, New York, Seoul, Singapore, Tokyo, Melbourne, Sydney, and London.

The industrial and commercial bank of China[80]

The Industrial and Commercial Bank of China ranks first among all commercial banks in the world in terms of annual profits and market capitalization. Along with the Bank of China, the Agricultural Bank of China, and China Construction Bank, it constitutes China's 'Big Four' of state-owned commercial banks. Its establishment can be traced back to the early 1980s. In September 1983, the State Council made the decision to spin the business of commercial banking off the People's Bank of China and have it function only as the central bank. Meanwhile, the spin-off business of commercial banking was transferred to a newly-established commercial bank named the 'Industrial and Commercial Bank of China'. Even though it is the youngest of the 'Big Four' group, the Industrial and Commercial Bank of China has developed at a rapid pace since its opening. According to existing statistics, in March 2010, 'it had assets of RMB 12.55 trillion, with over 18,000 outlets including 106 overseas branches and agents globally. In 2011, it ranked No. 7 on the Forbes Global 2000 list of the world's biggest public companies.'

In spite of its rapid development, the Industrial and Commercial Bank of China was afflicted by a huge number of non-performing loans for a long time. By the end of 2004, non-performing loans accounted for 19.1 per cent of its total assets. In order to polish up its balance sheet and prepare it for overseas listing, the Chinese Central Government took a series of measures including 'capital injections, asset transfers, and government-subsidized bad loan disposals that eventually cost more than $162 billion'. Among these measures, the $15 billion cash injected into the Industrial and Commercial Bank of China on 28 April 2005 came from China's massive foreign exchange reserves. In addition, China Huarong Asset Management Company was designated by the Chinese Central Government to help the Industrial and Commercial Bank of China dispose of part of its non-performing loans. By the end of 2005, the percentage of non-performing loans in its total assets had decreased sharply to 5 per cent.

The Industrial and Commercial Bank of China was simultaneously listed on both the Hong Kong Stock Exchange and the Shanghai Stock Exchange on 27 October 2006. At that time, it was the world's largest IPO, valued at $21.9 billion, surpassing the previous record of $18.4 billion set by Japan's NTT DoCoMo in 1998. In 2010, the Agricultural Bank of China broke the IPO record held by the Industrial and Commercial Bank of China, when it raised $22.1 billion from its IPO. The Industrial and Commercial Bank of China created the simultaneous listing model for the other three state-owned commercial banks to follow. As China's largest and most successful state-owned commercial bank, it is committed to speeding up the launch of innovative financial services for its clients and coming up with brand new models and ideas to overtake both its domestic and international competitors.

The relevant law for the regulation of the business lines of commercial banks in China is the Commercial Bank Law of the PRC. Pursuant to Article 3 of this law, the permissible business lines of Chinese commercial banks include taking deposits from the public, offering loans with different repayment periods, providing domestic and international settlement services, accepting and discounting negotiable instruments, issuing financial bonds, acting as an agent of issuing, cashing and underwriting governmental bonds, dealing in governmental bonds and financial bonds, conducting inter-bank lending, dealing or acting as an agent in dealing foreign currencies, issuing ATM cards, providing letters of credit service and their guarantees, acting as an agent in receiving payments and offering insurance services, and providing safe-deposit box services. Apparently, venture capital is excluded from the business lines of Chinese commercial banks, who should have been important institutional investors in this field, given the strong financial capability of the Big Four as described above.

Chinese insurance companies

The origin of the insurance sector of the PRC can be traced back to 20 October 1949, when the People's Insurance Company of China (PICC) was established by the new Chinese Central Government in the hope that the PICC would play an active role in the reconstruction of China's economy after it had been ravaged by wars for almost one hundred years. Since then, the development of the insurance sector of the PRC has been divided into two phases: the Maoist phase and the Dengist phase. These two phases will be elaborated on in the next section.

The Maoist phase (1949–1978)[81]

The Maoist phase ranged from 1949, when the PRC was founded, until 1978, when Mr. Xiaoping Deng regained the supreme leadership of the CPC after Chairman Zedong Mao passed away in 1976. During this time span of 30 years, the insurance industry of the PRC basically went through two distinct stages: the nationalization stage and the suspension stage.

On August 1949, Mr. Yun Chen, then director of the Financial and Economic Committee of the CPC, chaired the National Financial and Economic Affairs Meeting, during which a resolution to establish a state-owned insurance company was hammered out by all the delegates, and the People's Bank of China was instructed to take responsibility for setting up the company. One month later, the National Insurance Affairs Meeting was held, during which the policy of developing the insurance sector of the PRC was summarized as 'protecting national assets, securing production safety, promoting trade, stabilizing people's lives, raising funds from the public, and expanding national financial capability'. Right after the close of the meeting, Mr. Yibo Bo, then deputy director of the Financial and Economic Committee of the CPC, wrote an official letter to Mr. Hanchen Nan, then general manager of the People's Bank of China, issuing the instruction that 'the Central Committee of the CPC has approved of incorporating a state-owned insurance company as soon as possible'. With the strong support of the supreme leaders of the CPC, the first state-owned insurance company – the People's Insurance Company of China – was founded on 20 October 1949, which marked the birth of the insurance industry of the then newly-born PRC.

While busy with the setting-up of the PICC, the newly-born regime was getting down to nationalizing domestic privately-held insurance companies as well. This process lasted until 1958, by which time all domestic privately-held insurance companies were merged into the PICC, and foreign insurance companies completely suspended their Chinese operations. Along with the nationalization movement, the business of the PICC also entered its first period of boom. By the end of 1958, premiums collected by the PICC amounted to RMB 1.6 billion and the compensation made by the company grew to RMB 0.36 billion. Unfortunately, this boom time was suspended by the 'Great Leap' movement and the People's Communes movement, launched at the behest of Chairman Zedong Mao in 1958. During the National Finance and Trade Conference held by the State Council in October 1958 in Xi'an, the resolution was made that 'the function of insurance has already disappeared since the beginning of the People's Communes movement and therefore it ought to be suspended immediately'. From the beginning of 1959, the PICC was completely shut down by the State Council of the PRC. The suspension spanned the entire 10 years of the Cultural Revolution, and lasted until 1979, following the ending of the historic Third Plenary Session of the Eleventh Central Committee of the CPC which was held in December 1978. As a result of this politically motivated suspension, the Chinese insurance industry fell hugely behind its western counterparts.

The Dengist phase (1979-present)[82]

In December 1978, the Third Plenary Session of the Eleventh Central Committee of the CPC was successfully held in Beijing, an event which symbolized the ending of the exclusive policy of class struggle advocated by Chairman Zedong Mao during his 30 years ruling over the PRC, and declared the policy of reform and opening-up to be the new national strategy. In the context of reform and transition, a number of previously suspended sectors of the Chinese economy, including insurance, have reappeared. Between its restoration in 1979 and the present day, the Chinese insurance industry has already gone through three distinctive stages: the revival stage, the specialization stage, and the integration stage, each of which will be briefly introduced.

The revival stage (1979–1996)[83]

In 1979, the PICC re-opened to provide insurance service after 20 years' suspension. Until the middle of 1986, the PICC was the sole insurance company in China, and monopolized the Chinese insurance market. This situation was altered by the birth of a regional insurance company named 'Xinjiang Production and Construction Corps Agriculture and Animal Husbandry Insurance Company', which was incorporated in July 1986 with the approval of the People's Bank of China. In 2002, Xinjiang Production and Construction Corps Agriculture and Animal Husbandry Insurance Company was renamed 'China United Property Insurance Company Limited', an institution which is qualified to offer property insurance service nationwide under the approval of the China Insurance Regulatory Commission. Following the incorporation of Xinjiang Production and Construction Corps Agriculture and Animal

Husbandry Insurance Company, in 1987, the Bank of Communications also opened its insurance department. Four years later, the Bank of Communications switched this affiliated insurance unit to an independent company with its own legal personality and the new name of 'China Pacific Insurance Company', making it the second insurance institution with a license to operate comprehensive insurance business in the whole territory of the PRC.

Concomitant with the progress of China's economic reforms, in 1988, the People's Bank of China took the initiative of permitting the establishment of the first hybrid-ownership national insurance company, named 'Ping An Insurance (Group) Company of China' (Ping An Company). At that time, there were three main competitors, including the PICC, China Pacific Insurance Company, and Ping An Company, in the Chinese insurance sector. In 1992, AIA Group, a subsidiary of American International Group (AIG), went back to its original location – Shanghai – to incorporate a branch there, which became the first wholly foreign-owned insurance company in the PRC. Along with the opening of this branch, AIA Group also brought the concept of 'insurance salesmen' into the Chinese insurance sector, and trained the first generation of Chinese insurance salesmen. Subsequently, the practice of 'insurance salesmen' was quickly adopted by Chinese domestic insurance companies, marking a fundamental change in the whole insurance industry in China. On 30 June 1995, the Insurance Law of the PRC (Insurance Law) was enacted by the Standing Committee of the NPC. This law requires that any insurance company operating in China can only offer either property insurance or life insurance, not both. Since then, the Chinese insurance sector had entered into the specialty stage.

The specialty stage (1996–2003)

Pursuant to the specialty requirement of the Insurance Law, on 23 July 1996, the PICC was restructured into five companies including the PICC (Group), the PICC Property Insurance Company, the PICC Life Insurance Company, the PICC Re-insurance Company, and the PICC Overseas Branch. Among them, the PICC (Group) played the role of parent company, holding all the shares of the other four subsidiaries. Each of the subsidiaries was incorporated to sell a specific kind of insurance clearly stipulated by the Insurance Law. In the same year, the first batch of hybrid-ownership insurance companies were created following the enactment of the Insurance Law, which has made the Chinese insurance sector a more competitive market.

In November 1998, the China Insurance Regulatory Commission, which is responsible for regulating the Chinese insurance market, was formed by the State Council. Since then, the China Insurance Regulatory Commission has set up branches in each province of China to build up its seamless surveillance system. Meanwhile, the State Council dissolved the PICC (Group) and liberalized its four subsidiaries as independent and unrelated companies. The PICC Property Insurance Company has inherited the name of the 'PICC', and the PICC Life Insurance Company has been renamed the 'China Life Insurance Company' (China Life). The PICC Re-insurance Company and the PICC Overseas Branch have also been renamed, respectively, the 'China Insurance (Group) Corporation' and the PICC (Hong Kong). In 2002, China Life received an annual premium payment of RMB 128.7 billion, due to which it was listed in the Fortune 500 for the first time. One year later, the new PICC and China Life were floated on both the Hong Kong Stock Market and the New York Stock Market one after another. In particular, the floating of China Life represented the largest IPO that year. As vividly described by the media, the international financial market at the time was swept by the 'cyclone' of the Chinese insurance companies.

The universal stage (2003-present)[84]

Between 2003 and the present day, the PICC and China Life have taken the lead in pushing the Chinese insurance sector into the universal stage. Specifically, China Life set up its own assets management company in late 2003. Four years later, China Life landed successfully on the Shanghai Stock Exchange, becoming the first Chinese company listed in New York, Hong Kong, and mainland China. In 2009, the total assets of China Life reached RMB 1420 billion, accounting for 37.8 per cent of the aggregated assets of all Chinese insurance companies. In the same year, its domestic premium inflow was RMB 179.6 billion, accounting for 40.7 per cent of the entire market share. Meanwhile, its assets management company became the largest institutional investor in the Chinese capital market, managing RMB 1270 billion worth of financial assets. With the engine of fast growth and expansion, China Life was among both the Fortune 500 and the World Brand 500 for the first time that year.

In addition to China Life, the PICC has also used this strong momentum to expand itself into a universal insurance group company. In pursuit of this ambitious goal, the PICC opened a health insurance company, an assets management company, and an insurance brokerage company one after another. Driven by these initiatives, its annual premium inflow has also risen sharply. In 2008, for example, it received property insurance premiums of RMB 101.9 billion, making it the first Chinese property insurance company crossing the annual premium threshold of RMB 100 billion.

The above description summarizes the developmental process of the Chinese insurance sector. Along with fast growth, Chinese insurance companies have already become very important institutional investors in the Chinese capital market by investing the tremendous quantity of assets in their hands in various different fields. Specifically, pursuant to the latest version of the Insurance Law which was published by the Standing Committee of the NPC, insurance companies incorporated in China are allowed to invest their own assets in the form of deposits in banks, purchasing bonds, stocks of listed companies or shares of mutual funds, or the development of real estate. It is clear, however, that the above range of investment options is not satisfactory, at least as far as this researcher is concerned, because venture capital is not included, and in fact is strictly prohibited as an investment choice for insurance companies operating in China pursuant to a regulation entitled 'Provisional Administration Measures on the Usage of Insurance Assets', which explains the provisions of the amended Insurance Law in a more concrete and detailed way. As a result, insurance companies which could have been active players in the Chinese VC industry are still partitioned from this promising and lucrative area due to legal barriers.

Legal reform measures

Despite Chinese institutional investors, including pension funds, commercial banks, and insurance companies being financial giants, they have been prevented from entering the door of the Chinese venture capital industry due to legal barriers. In order to increase the fundraising sources for Chinese domestic venture capital and reinforce its ability to compete against foreign rivals, it will be necessary for the Chinese legislature and the Chinese Central Government to take swift action in removing these legal impediments. It is, however, also worth noting that liberalizing Chinese institutional investors to engage in domestic venture capital activities must co-ordinate effectively with the principle of prudence which governs the operation of these gigantic financial institutions. In other words, there must be a tailor-made legal cap applied to each institutional investor, to restrain its degree of involvement in the venture capital industry and ensure the prudence of its overall operations. The measures to reform relevant Chinese laws and regulations in this regard will be double-faceted. Firstly, the relevant laws and regulations, such as the Provisional Regulation of National Social Security Funds' Investment, the Commercial Bank Law of the PRC, and the Insurance Law of the PRC, ought to be revised to embrace venture capital as an investment area for institutional investors. Secondly, restraints ought to be incorporated into these laws and regulations to exercise control of governed institutional investors' participation in venture capital investments and maintain their prudent management.

Apart from the revision of state laws and regulations to allow Chinese institutional investors to involve themselves in the Chinese domestic venture capital industry, soft laws, including arm's length contracts, incentives, and monitoring mechanisms should also be devised by Chinese institutional investors to deal with their relationships with domestic venture capitalists and minimize these professionals' agency costs. The recent eye-catching case of CDH Fund explains this necessity to a large degree.

CDH Fund was previously the equity–investment division of China International Capital Corporation Limited. In 2001, the CSRC issued a regulation entitled 'Notice regarding Regulating the Engagement of Securities Companies in Venture Capital Investment' to ban securities companies like China International Capital Corporation Limited from engaging in venture capital activities. As a result, China International Capital Corporate Limited made the decision to spin off its equity-investment division. In 2002, the management team of the spin-off division, along with Temasek Holdings of Singapore, Zurich Insurance Group Limited, and China National Investment and Guaranty Corporation, set up CDH Fund.

Relying on the reputation of its founding shareholders, CDH Fund has quickly become a leading private equity company in China. In 2010, CDH Fund set up a private equity fund named 'Tianjin Dinghui Equity Investment Fund I (LLP)', with a focus on real estate development in Shanghai and Hangzhou. 'Tianjin Dinghui Equity Investment Fund I (LLP)' has been a success, with an annual profit margin of 15.55 per cent. Given this success, CDH Fund launched 'Tianjin Dinghui Equity Investment Fund II (LLP)', which also aimed at the real estate market, in 2012. Interestingly, the SSF acted as the biggest limited partner for both of these funds.

Recently, CDH Fund has come under the spotlight due to an ongoing dispute between one of its senior managers and a business intermediary. According to reports in the mainstream media in China, the dispute resulted from an accusation that the senior manager embezzled a business opportunity he was informed of by the inter-mediary for CDH Fund. Briefly, the senior manager of CDH Fund charged with the business embezzlement met the intermediary at a social occasion in 2010. After mutual introductions, the intermediary informed the senior manager of an investment project for exploiting ores in Mongolia. The senior manager verbally promised the intermediary in private that CDH Fund would pay the intermediary a commission of RMB 10 million if CDH Fund successfully engaged in the project of ore-exploitation. Soon after, CDH Fund decided to give up this project and consequently the verbally promised commission to the intermediary was aborted. According to the frustrated intermediary, however, the accused senior manager of CDH Fund, along with several other investors, went to Mongolia to carry out a field study on the project after CDH Fund announced its withdrawal. As a result, the so-far unsettled dispute has occurred, with the so-called 'business embezzlement' of the senior manager alleged by the intermediary.[85]

Although the facts of the dispute described above have not yet been investigated by any dispute-resolution institutions, the episode itself reveals the potential risks of agency collaboration, together with the engagement of Chinese institutional investors in the Chinese domestic venture capital market in the future. In other words, Chinese domestic venture capitalists may try to increase their own profits at the expense of venture investors, including institutional ones. Thus, soft laws, including arm's length contracts, incentives, and monitoring mechanisms should be devised by Chinese institutional investors to tackle the problem of interest divergence. In this regard, the operational model of Silicon Valley Bank offers us a good example.

Silicon Valley Bank (SVB) was incorporated in 1982, and its first office opened in 1983. In 2004, the bank set up international outlets in Bangalore and London. In 2005, it also launched branches in Beijing and Israel. In November 2012, the bank announced a half-and-half joint venture with Shanghai Pudong Development Bank (SPDB), providing capital to high-technology startups. SVB plans to use the Shanghai joint venture as a springboard to help it expand its business to other major Chinese cities.

SVB did not escape being hit by the 2008 financial crisis as other major financial institutions in America suffered. In December 2008, SVB declared that it would acquire $235 million in the form of loans from the US Treasury Department through the Troubled Asset Relief Program. In December 2009, SVB paid off this loan and bought back the outstanding stock pledges held by the US government, funding this through a stock sale of $300 million in November. In March 2011, SVB was awarded 'Bank of the Year' by the Ex-Im Bank. By October 2011, SVB had more than 1400 employees. By September 2012, it had offices in the United Kingdom, Israel, China, and India, plus more than 20 offices in the United States with total assets of $21.6 billion.

SVB focuses principally on two business lines. Firstly, it provides money for venture capital companies to set up venture capital funds. Secondly, it takes deposits from high-technology startups financed by venture capital funds for which SVB is a founder, by means of inserting a mandatory deposit-collection provision in investment contracts between investee startups and venture capital funds. It also offers additional services to these funded startups in order to retain them as clients as they mature beyond their startup phases. This operational strategy has the ability to reduce the self-interested behaviors of the venture capitalists SVB funds, because SVB can clearly see the cashflows, and thus the performance, of the funded startups selected by the relevant venture capitalists. Although the model of SVB can only be directly emulated by Chinese commercial banks who intend to engage in the Chinese venture capital sector, its implications – that soft laws including arm's length contracts, incentives, and monitoring mechanisms should be devised by Chinese institutional investors to tackle the problem of interest divergence – extend to other Chinese institutional investors harboring the same ambitions as Chinese commercial banks. In other words, legal reform of fundraising of Chinese domestic venture capital should be double-faceted: state laws and soft laws.[86]

Operation of Chinese venture capital: legal problems and reform measures

3

Operation of American venture capital

In the context of the cycle of venture capital, 'operation' refers principally to the injection of venture funds into selected start-ups.[87] For the sake of the success of joint ventures established both by venture capital and entrepreneurs, three aspects must be considered at this stage.[88] First, venture capitalists must determine what type of organization they use to inject venture funds into targeted start-ups. The significance of this question lies in the fact that venture investors, who are rational persons, will show different degrees of willingness to invest in the venture capital industry when they face different organizational arrangements adopted by venture capitalists to structure venture funds.[89] In turn, the different magnitudes of investment made by venture investors have a substantial influence on the sufficiency of the money pools under the management venture capital. Secondly, in order to convince themselves to contribute money to promising start-up companies, which are also associated with high uncertainty and great information asymmetry,[90] venture capitalists must work out the organizational and contractual mechanisms which they will apply to these portfolio companies for the purpose of minimising risk and harvesting their investment. Thirdly, venture capitalists must ensure that the management of start-ups is incentivized to perform at its best for the success of the venture, and to accept reduced control over the entities in return for pecuniary and non-pecuniary support from venture capital.[91] Essentially, the three aforementioned issues refer collectively to the selection and application of organizational and contractual incentives in the operation of venture capital.

With regard to the above three aspects, the operation of American venture capital has provided persuasive answers. First of all, most American venture capital funds are structured as limited partnerships.[92] Under this structure, venture investors serve as limited partners.[93] In terms of the legal rules governing limited partnerships in America, limited partners enjoy limited liability if they can abstain from exercising control over the critical elements of venture funds' business.[94] Correspondingly, virtually complete management power over venture capital is granted to venture capitalists who serve as general partners.[95] On the one hand, the balance of control between limited partners and general partners shows that investors need to rely on the skills and expertise of venture capitalists to make investments.[96] On the other hand, it also ensures that venture capitalists possess sufficient discretion to maximize investors' benefits using their knowledge and experience.[97] For the sake of minimizing agency costs resulting from control allocation, limited partnerships use compensation to guarantee the interests of general partners in line with those of limited partners. The bulk of general partners' compensation comes from a fixed share of ultimately realized profits of limited partnerships.[98] As a result, this compensation scheme creates incentives for venture capitalists to maximize the investment returns of venture funds. In addition, limited partnerships have limited lives, typically ten years, after which the partnerships must be dissolved and their assets returned to investors.[99] Apparently, the fixed termination provides a mechanism for prospective investors to estimate the abilities of venture capitalists, and their overall performance, by the time of liquidation.[100] Therefore, in order to remain in the venture capital sector, venture capitalists have incentives to lead the funds at hand to success before their dissolution. With regard to tax deduction, limited partnership income, in contrast with the dual taxation applicable to corporations, is not subject to taxation at the entity level.[101] In comparison with other organizational forms, the presence of the above features in limited partnerships boosts the willingness of venture investors to finance them. In 1980, 42.5 per cent of the investments made by venture capital in America were in those firms structured as limited partnerships. This number had increased substantially, to 81.2 per cent, by 1995.[102] Almost all of the foreign venture funds operating in China are limited partnerships, because their funds are mainly raised in the territories of their own countries.[103]

In order to minimize the high risks and agency costs concomitant with the start-up firms in which they invest, American venture capitalists commonly rely on staged financing, board representation, stock options, and convertible preferred stock.[104] Staged financing refers to the fact that the initial venture capital investment is generally not sufficient for portfolio firms to accomplish their overall business plans.[105] Subsequent injection of funds into these firms will occur only if certain landmarks spelled out in their business plans are achieved.[106] The mechanism of staged financing guarantees that venture capitalists can be promptly responsive to the high risks and high uncertainty associated with start-up companies, by granting themselves the right to withdraw.[107] At the same time, their option to withdraw also sends a negative signal to potential venture investors with the effect of deterring them from investing in 'black hole' projects.[108] Although staged financing shifts the decision making on the continuation of joint ventures from entrepreneurs to venture capitalists, it cannot provide monitoring of the daily conduct of portfolio firms' managers.[109] In response to this shortcoming, venture capitalists usually ask for a disproportionate representation on, or even control of, their portfolio companies' boards of directors.[110] With this power, they are able to effectively monitor the day-to-day decisions taken by managers.[111] Another means of addressing agency costs utilized by American venture capital is the use of stock options as the principal part of managers' compensation.[112] Under this system, entrepreneurs undoubtedly have a strong incentive to strengthen the performance of portfolio companies and to increase the value of the shares they own. Likewise, by accepting low cash salaries in return for stock options, other management members also make their earnings largely dependent on the performance of portfolio companies, which they operate jointly with entrepreneurs.[113] In addition to linking the compensation of management to the success of joint ventures, the use of stock options can maintain the continuous commitment of the management team, because their stakes will be forfeited if they quit prior to certain specified dates.[114] The final tool on which American venture capitalists principally rely is convertible preferred stock. By making their investment in exchange for a certain amount of convertible preferred stock, issued by portfolio companies, venture capital funds profit from the conversion of their preferred stock into common stock when the portfolio companies are successful, and they bear disproportionately less risk than entrepreneurs should these companies fail.[115] Moreover, convertible preferred stock is subject to the terms governing liquidation preference, redemption right, and anti-dilution protection.[116] Liquidation preference gives priority to venture capitalists in the process of allocating liquidated assets, should portfolio companies go bankrupt.[117] Redemption right reinforces the liquidity of venture capitalists in the event of barely passable performance by portfolio companies.[118] Anti-dilution protection ensures that venture capitalists can protect their interests against contingencies that cause a value-dilutive effect.[119] Finally, American venture capitalists resort to a combination of stock options and the exit mechanism for the purpose of stimulating the management's willingness to perform at its best for the success of the joint venture and, simultaneously, to accept reduced control over the venture in return for monetary and non-monetary support from venture capital.[120] Given that exit is also the final stage of venture capital investment, it will be discussed in the next chapter.

The incentive mechanisms set out above, while prevailing in American venture capital, are comparatively undeveloped in Chinese domestic venture capital. The following section will attempt to demonstrate that this lack of development can be largely ascribed to state laws or soft laws, which maintain traditions herein.

Operation of Chinese domestic venture capital

As mentioned above, American venture capital relies on limited partnerships, stock options, and convertible preferred stocks to control uncertainty, information asymmetry, and agency costs associated with portfolio startup companies. By contrast, none of these incentive mechanisms are well-developed under the current Chinese legal framework.

Limited partnerships

Proposals in favor of transplanting limited partnerships to China by legislation have been put forward by a group of Chinese scholars and progressive government officials since the 1990s.[121] In a lecture addressing the audience of the People's University of China, Professor Ping Jiang, former principal of the China University of Political Science and Law, confirmed that the drafting team prepared a chapter entitled 'Limited Partnership' when they drew up the Partnership Enterprise Law of the PRC (Partnership Law) in 1997.[122] This chapter, however, was deleted after the final draft of the Partnership Law was presented to the Standing Committee of the NPC for final approval.[123] According to a senior member of the NPC, the reason for deleting that chapter was the non-existence of limited partnerships in Chinese commercial practice at that time.[124] He also said that the legislature would consider adding limited partnerships into the Partnership Law if this type of business organization was subsequently utilized by practitioners.[125]

Early in 2006, the CPC Central Committee and the State Council reached a strategic decision on the establishment of an innovative society.[126] In order to cater to this political slogan, the Standing Committee of the NPC amended the Partnership Law by enabling the formation of limited partnerships.[127] This change seemed to represent progress. Due to inertia, however, or to the traditional control exercised by the state over SOEs, especially state-controlled listed companies, the legislature eroded the freedom of limited partnership contracts. Pursuant to Article 61 of the Revised Partnership Law, the number of limited partners is limited to 49.[128] This mandatory cap has significantly restricted the fundraising capabilities of this organizational form in China.[129]

Staged financing and board representation

Evidence on the use of staged financing by Chinese domestic venture capital emanates from an interview with a venture capitalist affiliated to a provincial government.[130] According to his explanation, staged financing is a common tool used by government venture capital for its portfolio companies.[131] He adds, however, that it is a formality with little efficacy, because most projects in which government venture capital invests are actually selected by senior government officials, which means that government venture capitalists must continuously inject money into these 'lucky dogs' for the purpose of pandering to their seniors' vanity, even if the portfolio companies do not meet the requirements for the next financing round. The statement of this venture capitalist is consistent with earlier empirical research. According to that research, which took place between 2000 and 2002, the sample of government venture capital studied nominally used staged financing for its investee start-ups, but seldom carried out strict and thorough evaluations on the basis of which it could be decided whether to offer the next stage of financing.[132] The consistency of these two pieces of evidence demonstrates that staged financing will continue to malfunction when used in government venture capital as long as the operational model described by the venture capitalist above is still in place. Correspondingly, it can be deduced that the persistent malfunctioning of government venture capital limits the potential of staged financing to enhance the performance of investee start-ups. This conclusion has already been verified by other empirical research, showing that the staged financing adopted by the sample of government venture capital studied did not reinforce the performance of its portfolio start-ups from 2003 to 2012.[133] More importantly, the inappropriate intervention in the operation of government venture capital by government officials is caused by inertia, or the tradition of state entrepreneurialism, which has principally been maintained through state-controlled listed companies. Therefore, the substantive malfunctioning of staged financing in government venture capital can be linked to the tradition of Chinese governmental control. Although evidence reflecting the use of staged financing in domestic private venture capital is not available at the time of this research, it is fair to say that the case of government venture capital essentially mirrors the profile of this mechanism in the overall Chinese domestic venture capital industry, given that government venture capital represents the majority of this industry.

With regard to board representation, the interviewee mentioned above confirms that government venture capital always asks for board membership of portfolio companies. However, he states that board representation is aimed at satisfying the demands of government officials to be regarded as decision makers, rather than at obtaining information from the funded firms and monitoring their performance. Based on the above analysis it is not difficult to understand his statement. On the one hand, the government official's desire to give the impression of being at the center of a business is the inevitable by-product of state entrepreneurism. On the other hand, it is predictable that few venture capitalists in government venture capital actually wish to perform the surveillance duty in these 'guanxi' firms, for fear of displeasing their seniors. The interviewee's explanation is supported by more recent empirical research showing that, between 2000 and 2010, the sample of government venture capital firms studied usually placed delegates on the board of directors of their portfolio companies, but that these delegates were not proactive in monitoring and in collecting information about the performance of those companies.[134] This research conjectured that the passivity or indifference of delegate directors representing government venture capital in portfolio companies could perhaps be ascribed to the fact that government venture capital generally chooses the pre-IPO phase to inject capital into investee companies, thereby deviating from the early-stage investment focused on by authentic venture capital.[135] This conjecture, however, has been disproved by other recent empirical research, which shows that government venture capital is inclined to become substantially involved in early-stage investment.[136] Hence, the much more plausible reason for the indifference is the one described by the interviewee. As set out above, the limited effectiveness of government officials as well as venture capitalists in government venture capital is, to a large extent, ascribed to the influence of the tradition of state entrepreneurship. Also, by and large, board representation in government venture capital primarily represents a nod to the status quo in the overall Chinese domestic venture capital industry, due to government venture capital's leading position.

Convertible preferred stocks

The first Company Law of the PRC was promulgated in 1993 (Company Law 1993) for the purpose of the corporatization of traditional SOEs.[137] Through corporatization, the CPC and Chinese Central Government intended to privatize small and medium-sized SOEs and to reform and keep control of big and key ones through the mechanisms of modern corporate governance. This objective determined that Company Law 1993 included plenty of mandatory provisions which should, in the spirit of modern company law, have been discretionary ones.[138]

One aspect of the rigidity of Company Law 1993 was its provision regarding the distribution of profits among shareholders. In accordance with Article 33 and Article 177 of the law, profits were divided pro rata among shareholders on the basis of their shareholdings. This stipulation denied the existence of convertible preferred stocks, because the owners of these types of securities receive a fixed-rate dividend which was not determined by the level of their shareholdings. In the decade following the promulgation of Company Law 1993, and prior to its revision in 2005, a group of progressive government officials and scholars appealed to the Chinese legislature to amend the above two articles, and to add some new ones for the purpose of legalizing the use of preferred stocks.[139] The target of all these proposals, however, was the common shares held by the state in state-controlled listed companies, which meant that this group suggested substituting preferred stocks for the common ones.[140] Consequently, their petition did not obtain a positive response from the authorities, because decision makers thought that preferred stocks which were featured with restricted voting rights would undermine the state's control over state-controlled listed companies. Therefore, before the latest amendments of the Company Law 1993 became effective in 2006, common stocks naturally became the predominant investment vehicle of Chinese domestic venture capital, if not the only one.

With the rapid development of China's market economy and the increasing weight of privately held enterprises in the whole of society, more and more interested groups criticized Company Law 1993 for its stiffness.[141] Ultimately, after separate minor revamps in 1999 and 2004, the NPC overhauled it in 2005 to satisfy the needs of other participants in the economy.[142] With regard to profit distribution, pursuant to Article 35 and Article 167 of the amended Company Law, dividing profits among shareholders takes place not only on the basis of shareholdings. Other means permitted by articles of incorporation are also accepted by the new company law. This change has laid the legal ground for the use of convertible preferred stocks. Immediately after this modification, echoing the encouragement of innovation from the CPC and the Central Government,[143] ten ministries and committees of the State Council jointly enacted a regulation entitled 'Interim Measures for the Administration of Startup Investment Enterprises'.[144] As a result of this regulation, venture capital is finally allowed to take advantage of convertible preferred stocks.[145] This should have been a boost for Chinese domestic venture capital. However, these governmental agencies have not yet explained the use of this financial instrument, such as its issuance procedure or principal terms, in detail. Consequently, Chinese domestic venture capital is yet to apply these new rules to its investments.

Stock options

As demonstrated above, rigidity was a character of Company Law 1993. Stock options as an incentive mechanism were not among its stipulations. In addition, Article 149 of the ruling prohibited companies from purchasing their own stocks except to reduce registered capital or merge with other companies which held their shares. This provision made it impossible for companies to reserve stocks for the purpose of stock options.

With the deepening development of SOE reform, the CPC and the Chinese Central Government realized that it was necessary to introduce stock options as an incentive mechanism to supplement the control of governance institutions.[146] In 1999, the

Fifteenth CPC Central Committee passed a document entitled 'Decisions on SOEs Reform'.[147] In this document, the CPC Central Committee cautiously permitted a pilot trial of stock options in SOEs.[148] Since then, some experiments have been carried out, mainly in state-controlled listed companies located in several big cities.[149] However, because of the above legal barriers and the government's affinity with control, these endeavors have not been successful.[150] Here, the 'Wuhan model' is taken as an example for illustrative purposes.[151] In this model, if a state-controlled listed company decided to award 'stock options' to a manager, the Wuhan State-owned Assets Administration Company would purchase the company's stocks from the secondary market with the manager's salaries. The stocks would not be awarded to the manager in a lump sum. Instead, within a fixed return period, the stocks would be granted to the manager on a yearly basis. If the performance of the manager was not satisfactory in a certain year within the return period, the due stock amount in that year would be expropriated by the Wuhan State-owned Assets Administration Company. A glance at the Wuhan model clearly demonstrates that its so-called 'stock options' operated very differently from legitimate stock options. They were more of a penalty and restriction on managers than an incentive. Hence, this approach inevitably ended in failure.

Even though the amended Company Law does in principle permit the use of stock options by Chinese business companies, in practice they are currently the privilege of Chinese listed companies, pursuant to a regulation entitled 'Administrative Methods of the Use of Stock Options in Chinese Listed Companies (Provisional)', which was enacted by the CSRC on 31 December 2005 and came into effect on 1 January 2006. As a result, Chinese domestic venture capital is still waiting for approval from the regulatory agency before applying it to investee startup companies.

Legal reform measures

On the basis of the analysis in the second part of this book, it is evident that state laws or soft laws, which primarily uphold tradition, have already suppressed the efficacy of the aforementioned tools, which are necessary for Chinese domestic venture capital to manage the multiple risks inherent in financing portfolio companies. In order to level the playing field for Chinese domestic venture capital, legal reform measures must be taken in a timely manner. Specifically, the Standing Committee of the NPC should remove the cap restricting the number of partners in a Chinese limited partnership to 49, a move which would substantially enhance the fundraising ability of this type of business entity in China. In addition, now that convertible preferred stocks and stock options are permissible for Chinese companies pursuant to the amended Chinese company law, the CSRC ought to make departmental ordinances to specify the procedure for the issuance of convertible preferred stocks and stock options by Chinese companies, especially limited liability ones, in detail. Without a set of issuance procedures, convertible preferred stocks and stock options are valuable financial instruments only on paper for startup companies backed by Chinese domestic venture capital. Lastly, the CPC and the Chinese Central Government should continue pushing Chinese political reform forward, with the ultimate mission of establishing a service-oriented government instead of the current state-entrepreneurism model. Only by eliminating the ingrained tradition of governments' undue intervention into economic activities carried out by market players, such as government venture capital, can the efficacy of staged financing and board representation be genuinely enjoyed by these business players.

Exit of Chinese venture capital: legal problems and reform measures

4

Exit channels of American venture capital

In the developmental history of American venture capital, the National Association of Securities Dealers Automated Quotations (NASDAQ) has undoubtedly played a vital role, by encouraging the exit of investors through IPOs.[152] As mentioned above, American venture funds are generally structured as limited partnerships, with a life span of around ten years.[153] This life limitation provides a benchmark against which venture investors can judge the skills of venture capitalists.[154] Therefore, in order to accumulate positive track records for future fundraising, venture capitalists need to achieve an exit from successful portfolio companies before the deadline. After ten years, even successful venture enterprises are still too young and small-scale to satisfy the listing rules of American main boards, at a time when venture capital firms plan to opt out. Hence, to facilitate venture capital's withdrawal from portfolio companies by means of IPOs, it became necessary to establish a stock market with listing rules which can match the relatively low level of success of these entities. The NASDAQ fulfils this function.

With regard to the initial listing requirements of the NASDAQ Capital Market,[155] applicant companies are eligible to be listed only if they meet one of its three standards – the equity standard, the market value of listed securities standard, or the net income standard.[156] Each of the three standards are set relatively low, with fairly loose criteria to measure potential listed companies. Taking the equity standard as an example, its main indicators include: (1) stockholders' equity of 5 million US dollars, (2) market value of publicly-held shares of 15 million US dollars, (3) publicly-held shares of 1 million US dollars, (4) and operating history of 2 years.[157] There is no requirement for net income from continuing operations. Together with the rapid procedure for attaining listing approval adopted by the Securities and Exchange Commission (SEC),[158] this kind of lower listing requirement enables American venture capital to exit smoothly from successful portfolio companies through IPOs. Statistics tell us that, between 1992 and 2002, the number of IPOs of venture-capital-backed companies on the NASDAQ was 1,721, and the amount of money raised was 107.24 billion US dollars.[159]

One may question the NASDAQ by highlighting the severe slumping of its index after the bursting of the 'dot-com bubble' in 2000.[160] In the opinion of this writer, this kind of argument is unreasonable. Undeniably, the NASDAQ Composite Index went through a drastic fall during the dot-com disaster.[161] But it is unfair to estimate the contribution of a stock market purely on the basis of a temporary fluctuation. Any objective attitude towards the NASDAQ ought to focus on its past and future. Historically, the NASDAQ has played a critical role in the development of American venture capital. To a large extent, without the NASDAQ, the vibrant venture capital sector in America may not have appeared. In the future, by improving regulation for the continuous listing, plus restoring investors' confidence,[162] the NASDAQ will continue to support the success of American venture capital by providing an efficient exit channel.

By contrast, foreign venture capital which makes investments in China seldom takes advantage of Chinese domestic stock markets for the purpose of exiting from successful portfolio companies, due to China's stringent foreign currency policy.[163] This impediment, however, has not created fundamental obstacles to the accomplishment of liquidity through IPOs, because access is available to overseas Growth Enterprise Markets (GEMs), such as the NASDAQ.

Generally speaking, in order to circumvent approval from the CSRC,[164] foreign venture capital and its Chinese portfolio companies rely on special purpose vehicles (SPVs) to achieve indirect listings on overseas GEMs.[165] SPVs are usually incorporated in offshore jurisdictions, such as the British Virgin Islands (BVI), Cayman Islands, or Bermuda, by the controlling shareholders of the aforementioned Chinese companies backed by foreign venture capital.[166] After their incorporation, SPVs purchase all the outstanding shares of venture-capital-sponsored companies with their own stocks.[167] Then they file applications to float with one of the overseas GEMs.[168] If their requests are approved by GEMs, foreign venture capital shareholders can fulfil their exit through IPOs.

In 2006, six Chinese ministries, including the Ministry of Commerce (MOC), the SASAC, the CSRC, the State Administration of Taxation (SAT), the State Administration for Industry and Commerce (SAIC), and the State Administration of Foreign Currency (SAFE), collectively enacted a regulation entitled 'Interim Provisions on the Takeover of Domestic Enterprises by Foreign Investors'.[169] Pursuant to this regulation, SPVs are required to obtain approval from the MOC before they purchase the shares of affiliated domestic companies.[170] Apparently, this requirement has added extra costs to the traditional SPV model for the exit of foreign venture capital, because administrative approval is time-consuming and uncertain.[171] This shouldn't, however, be taken to mean that for foreign venture capital practitioners in China, the SPV approach has reached a dead end. As Article 2 of the regulation defines them, 'domestic companies' refer to all companies incorporated in the jurisdiction of China, except foreign-invested ones.[172] Therefore, in order to avoid the approval requirement when relying on SPVs to fulfil an exit, foreign venture capital firms simply need to convert their Chinese portfolio companies into foreign-invested companies.[173] This practice has already been implicitly recognized by the MOC after a company named 'Zhongwang' was successfully listed on the GEM of Hong Kong following this conversion.[174]

In contrast, Chinese domestic venture capital which has not earned a reputation in the global financial markets is reluctant to depend on overseas GEMs as a liquidity channel, because its portfolio companies lack attractiveness to foreign investors in comparison with those backed by foreign venture capital which is already prestigious worldwide.[175] Consequently, the exit of Chinese domestic venture capital is tightly connected to Chinese domestic stock markets.

Exit channels of Chinese domestic venture capital

Currently, Chinese domestic stock markets comprise three parts: the Main Board, the Small and Medium-sized Enterprise Board (SME Board), and the newly-established GEM. According to official statements, the presence of these three parts has enabled China to fulfil the mission of establishing a multi-tier domestic stock market.[176] Next, the three boards will be analyzed one by one in order to demonstrate that none of them have assumed the duty of providing a smooth exit channel for Chinese domestic venture capital, due to the impediments put in place by the relevant laws, regulations, and policies.

Main Boards

Generally speaking, the Main Board of a stock market aims to provide a financing channel for well-established companies. Therefore, it usually maintains a high set of listing standards, which are difficult for successful venture-capital-backed companies to satisfy when venture capital is preparing to exit from them. Consequently, the Main Board is not aimed primarily at fundraising for small-sized and medium-sized companies, or for the exit of venture capital from these firms. In some cases, however, when venture capitalists have been planning an exit, their portfolio companies have been so fully feathered that they have reached the listing criteria of Main Boards. Hence, venture capital firms and their collaborative entrepreneurs may prefer to list their companies directly on Main Boards in order to raise more money and reap more profits. When this happens, an efficient and fair Main Boards should be able to satisfy such a demand. In other words, a well-devised Main Board can present equal opportunities for potential qualified companies, including venture-capital-backed ones, to be floated. Unfortunately, this quality of equal opportunity is still absent from the Main Boards of Chinese domestic stock markets.

The underlying intention of the CPC and the State Council to establish the Shanghai Stock Exchange and the Shenzhen Stock Exchange was to facilitate fundraising for moribund SOEs.[177] The authorities could not, however, express this intention in a straightforward manner because they had to nominally accommodate the interests of privately-held enterprises under the umbrella of fairness and equality.[178] Therefore, in order to ensure that as many SOEs could be listed as possible, the authorities placed the power of listing approval in their own hands from the beginning.[179]

From the inception of the Chinese stock markets until the year 2000, the Chinese Central Government implemented a dual-control policy regarding the listing of enterprises on the Shanghai Stock Exchange and the Shenzhen Stock Exchange.[180]

Under this policy, the related units of the State Council determined a listing volume cap and a listing number cap each year.[181] Then, each provincial government was assigned a quota for choosing enterprises to be listed.[182] Thus, in this listing approval system, provincial governments were the actual decision makers, and they inevitably preferred to select the SOEs located in their areas as the listed candidates.[183] On the one hand, the dual-control policy created the first batch of state-controlled listed companies, which in turn deepened the incentive for the authorities to maintain the power of listing approval to preferentially enlarge this category.[184] On the other hand, the selection of listed companies through an administrative approach determined that the quality of those enterprises was usually given inadequate attention by decision makers.[185] Therefore, for the sake of the sustainable development of the Chinese stock markets, it was necessary to reform the dual-control policy.

From 2001 to 2003, the Chinese Central Government and the CSRC replaced the dual-control policy with a dual-recommendation policy.[186] According to this policy, provincial governments and qualified securities companies were responsible for selecting candidate enterprises to be listed on the Shanghai Stock Exchange or the Shenzhen Stock Exchange.[187] Simply speaking, provincial governments were authorized to determine a shortlist of potential listing companies.[188] Then, those companies struck contracts with qualified securities companies to receive pre-listing assistance.[189] Finally, the qualified securities companies recommended the companies whose performance was satisfactory during the assistance period to the CSRC for ultimate approval.[190] From this brief description it can be seen that, compared with the dual-control policy, the dual-recommendation policy showed greater concern with the quality of listed companies, by involving securities companies with expert knowledge to help the candidate enterprises reach the listing standards. Due to the SOE-oriented nature of the Chinese stock markets,[191] however, provincial governments maintained the power to determine the shortlists of enterprises to be listed in accordance with the dual-recommendation policy. In addition, securities companies were incentivized to recommend the enterprises favored by local governments to the CSRC, in order to acquire more underwriting opportunities from local governments in the future. Consequently, under the dual-recommendation system, SOEs still possessed considerable advantages in the process of attaining listings.

Since 2004, for the purpose of further improving the quality of listed companies, the CSRC has made securities companies liable for their recommendations if the recommended companies are subsequently identified to be inconsistent with the listing standards.[192] This change, however, has not fundamentally affected the powers of listing selection held by local governments, because both the vested interests and potential ones present incentives for local governments to lobby central government to keep this power.[193] Hence, the main boards of Chinese stock markets continue to favor SOEs.

This introduction to the evolution of Chinese listing approval policies reveals the fact that the two main boards in China are not able to provide a smooth and fair exit channel for Chinese domestic venture capital firms, even if their portfolio companies reach the listing standards. Just as the venture capitalist from a Chinese domestic venture capital firm argued, venture capital hardly has the opportunity to approach Chinese main boards, which are the traditional turf of giant SOEs.[194] Perhaps that may explain why, of 120 newly-listed companies on the main boards of the Shanghai Stock Exchange and the Shenzhen Stock Exchange in 2007, only two were venture-capital-backed.[195]

The SME board

The SME Board belonging to the Shenzhen Stock Exchange was launched by the State Council in May 2005. This SME Board was viewed as an interim form of the GEM by the Chinese authorities.[196] Its mission is to provide an exit channel for Chinese domestic venture capital, and to establish a convenient fundraising environment for SMEs, especially for high technology ones. Objectively speaking, the presence of the SME Board has to some degree alleviated the financing difficulties confronted by SMEs.[197] However, it also inevitably diverts a portion of capital which should have flowed into the main boards and in turn threatens the vested interests of state-controlled listed companies. Chinese governments are not willing to ignore competition from SMEs, most of which are privately held against state-controlled listed companies in the Chinese stock markets.[198] Consequently, in order to weaken the effect of capital diversion of the SME Board, the Chinese Central Government has completely transplanted the listing standards, the listing approval procedure, and even the policy of equity division of the Chinese main boards to the SME Board.[199] Therefore, the real function of the SME Board is unlikely to be consistent with the missions mentioned above. As this part of the book is focused only on the exits of Chinese domestic venture capital, it will principally analyze how this transplantation has disabled the SME Board from normal functioning in this regard.

The listing standards of the SME Board include several key accounting indicators for candidate firms. First, the pre-listing shares of the candidate firm must be worth above RMB 30 million.[200] Second, the net profits of the candidate company in each of the past three accounting years must be positive, and their overall amount must be greater than RMB 30 million.[201] Third, the overall cash flow of the candidate company in the past three accounting years must be above RMB 50 million, or its overall revenue in the past three accounting years must be above RMB 0.3 billion.[202] Fourth, at the end of the final quarter of the immediately previous accounting year, the ratio of the candidate company's intangible assets to its net assets must not be above 20 per cent, and it must not have losses without compensation.[203] The aggregation of these accounting criteria determines that only capital-concentrated SMEs, which are usually from the manufacturing industry, possess the scale and capability to satisfy the high listing requirements. Numerous high technology SMEs barely reach the threshold specified by the SME Board. Consequently, for the exit of Chinese domestic venture capital through the SME Board, the impact of the prohibitive listing standards is twofold. First, Chinese domestic venture capital firms can rarely achieve an exit from high technology companies backed by them via the SME Board. Second, if Chinese domestic venture capital firms hope to rely on the SME Board for the purpose of exit, they must invest in companies in the manufacturing industry. Taking into account the fact that venture capital is not willing to become massively

Table 4.1 **An overview of listed companies on the SME Board of the Shenzhen Stock Exchange, 2004 to 2007**

Industry	2004		2005		2006		2007	
	VC-backed	Non-VC-backed	VC-backed	Non-VC-backed	VC-backed	Non-VC-backed	VC-backed	Non-VC-backed
Agriculture	0	0	1	0	0	2	0	1
Mining	0	0	0	0	0	0	1	1
Manufacture	9	25	2	7	8	28	20	56
Public Utilities	0	0	0	1	0	0	0	0
Construction	0	0	0	0	0	3	1	1
Transportation and Storage	0	1	0	1	0	0	0	0
Information Technology	0	1	0	0	3	4	4	4
Sales and Retails	0	1	0	0	0	1	0	1
Finance and Insurance	0	0	0	0	0	0	0	1
Real Estate	0	0	0	0	0	0	0	2
Social Services	0	1	0	0	0	2	4	2
Media and Entertainment	0	0	0	0	0	0	0	1
Others	0	0	0	0	0	1	0	0
Total	9	29	3	9	11	41	30	70

Source: China Venture Capital Yearbook (2008).[204]

involved in traditional industry, the ratio of venture-capital-backed listed companies on the SME Board is low. The existing empirical evidence confirms these judgments. According to the data in Table 4.1, it is clear that the overwhelming majority of venture-capital-backed listed companies on the SME Board came from the manufacturing industry between 2004 and 2007. Meanwhile, as Table 4.2 shows, the quantity of venture-capital-backed listed companies among all the listed companies on the SME Board was only 26.2 per cent across the above-mentioned four years. In addition to the listing standards, the listing approval procedure of the SME Board, which features administrative selection as described previously, can also filter out a portion of venture-capital-backed candidates of high quality and extend listing opportunities to established SOEs which are not named in listings quotas on the main boards. Last year, one of the author's relatives, who was vice mayor of a county in China, told him that a large-scale state-owned steel company located in her county had obtained approval from the provincial government and CSRC to be listed on the SME Board after it failed to lobby for an entrance ticket to the main boards.

As for the policy of equity division, it once made the exit of Chinese domestic venture capital through the SME Board impossible. In accordance with the requirements

Table 4.2 **Numbers of listed companies on the SME Board of the Shenzhen Stock Exchange, 2004 to 2007**

Year	Numbers of IPOs					
	VC-backed		Non-VC-backed		Total IPOs	
	Numbers	Percentage	Numbers	Percentage	Numbers	Percentage
2004	9	24.32	28	75.68	37	100
2005	3	25	9	75	12	100
2006	11	21.15	41	78.85	52	100
2007	30	30	70	70	100	100
Total	53	26.2	149	73.8	202	100

Source: China Venture Capital Yearbook (2008).[205]

of the policy, shares held by the state and legal persons were prohibited from being traded on the secondary market. As a matter of fact, most Chinese domestic venture capital firms are structured as companies, which are deemed legal persons by the relevant PRC laws.[206] Therefore, the policy of equity division meant that Chinese domestic venture capital was not able to achieve exit via the SME Board, even if the relevant portfolio companies had been successfully listed there. In 2005, in order to rescue the Chinese main boards from the brink of collapse, the CSRC launched a reform of the policy of equity division.[207] Benefiting from this reform, shares held by legal persons are now permitted to be traded on the SME Board.[208] Objectively speaking, the abolishment of the equity division policy has promoted the exit of Chinese domestic venture capital through the SME Board. However, it also reflects the fact that Chinese stock markets are still SOE-oriented, and Chinese domestic venture capital is at most a 'free rider' on policies in favor of state-controlled listed companies. Thus, without resetting the mission of the Chinese stock markets, the effects of any reforms at a technical level are inevitably limited.

The GEM

After ten years' discussion and waiting, the Chinese GEM was eventually launched by the Chinese Central Government in May 2009. In comparison with the main boards and the SME Board, the listing standards and listing approval procedures of the GEM are more suitable for the reality of high technology venture enterprises. For example, with regard to accounting conditions, the GEM requires only that candidate enterprises have been continuously profitable during the two years prior to listing. Net profits in the period must be above RMB 10 million, the trend of profitability must be lasting, and net assets must have been above RMB 20 million at the end of the last quarter of the immediately previous accounting year.[209] In addition, when determining listing approval, the pre-approval of provincial governments is excluded.[210] Therefore, the GEM is theoretically an ideal exit channel for Chinese domestic venture capital. However, this function of the Chinese GEM has not yet been fully exploited.

As we know, the main boards of stock markets play the role of providing a fundraising platform for established companies. Different from the main boards, the GEM is principally responsible for the exit of venture capital from successful portfolio firms. The fundraising of companies is merely the 'side product' of this kind of exit. The rationale underlying this orientation of the GEM is that the potential of the venture capital industry for financing SMEs is much higher than that of the GEM. Therefore, by acting as an exit channel for venture capital, the GEM can stimulate potentially huge capital flow into the venture capital industry, and the adequate fundraising of venture capital can in turn satisfy the financing demands of thousands of SMEs.[211] Unfortunately, this rationale has not been fully realized by the Chinese authorities because they are primarily focused on the financing function of the Chinese main boards. Consequently, they are inclined to label the GEM a market of financing as well. This means that the Chinese authorities do not pay much attention to the exits of Chinese domestic venture capital via the GEM; instead they care more about listing as many enterprises as possible. Even though it is rather limited at present, due to the very short history of the Chinese GEM, the existing empirical evidence can basically prove the above analysis. After checking the 10 biggest shareholders of the first 28 listed companies on the GEM, it has been found that the 10 biggest shareholders of 10 companies among the 28 listed companies do not include venture capital. In addition, some venture capital institutions invested in 11 of the 18 venture-capital-backed companies directly before their listings, for the purpose of being 'free riders'.[212] Just as Zhongting Wu, who is the CEO of Beijing Huaqi Information Digital Technology Corporation, said, there were few venture capital firms which actively got in touch with her before her company applied to be listed on the GEM. After it filed the application, however, many venture capital firms approached her to invest.[213] Therefore, among 28 listed companies, the authentic exit of Chinese domestic venture capital from successful portfolio firms accounts for at most 25 per cent.[214]

Legal reform measures

In order to genuinely allow Chinese stock markets to assume the responsibility of providing fair and efficient channels for the exit of Chinese domestic venture capital from successful portfolio companies, a series of legal reforms to relevant regulations, as follows, must be conducted as quickly as possible. First, the CSRC ought to convert the current listing approval system to a listing registration system. In other words, when it reviews listing applications from candidate companies, the CSRC should judge only the track record of compliance of these companies, instead of predicting their investment values and market prospects by consulting relevant provincial governments and ministries, as it has done thus far. By doing this, the listing fairness of the Main Board in China will be improved, benefiting both venture-capital-backed enterprises and similar ones without strong governmental backgrounds. Secondly, the CSRC should address the fact that the listing requirements for the SME Board have been replicated from the Main Board, and should lower these requirements down to a reasonable level so as to enhance the possibilities for Chinese domestic venture capital to exit through this channel. Lastly, with the precondition of maintaining fairness to all candidate companies, the CSRC should encourage the GEM to play the role of the leading exit channel for Chinese domestic venture capital, rather than focusing only on the number of enterprises floated by the GEM. In other words, the CSRC ought to release a clear signal that it encourages Chinese domestic venture capital to make use of the GEM as a principal exit channel. As long as the GEM really opens the door for Chinese domestic venture capital to exit, the fundraising problem of Chinese SMEs will be alleviated accordingly.

Conclusions: How long will it take for reform to take place in China?

Dispersal of the ownership of state-controlled listed companies

In China, there exist two types of state-controlled listed companies. One type refers to those listed companies which are in the charge of the SASAC of the Chinese Central Government, and which are accordingly known as central state-controlled listed companies. The other type refers to those which are administered by the local SASACs of Chinese local governments, and are correspondingly dubbed local state-controlled listed companies. Central state-controlled listed companies are generally much larger than local ones. In terms of their business activities, central state-controlled listed companies are usually engaged in infrastructures and industries closely related to national security, such as the invention of sophisticated weapons, while local ones regularly operate in more competitive industries. 998 local state-controlled listed companies, and 194 central ones, were listed on the Chinese domestic stock market by the end of 2006.[215]

Given the very important role played by these companies in the stable reign of the CPC in China, leaders of the SASAC of the Chinese Central Government have stressed repeatedly that the majority blocks of shares held by the state in central state-controlled listed companies will never be significantly decreased.[216] Thus, it is highly unlikely that the concentrated ownership of central state-controlled listed companies will be substantively dispersed, at least within the short-term. To the contrary, the ownership of local state-controlled listed companies has been increasing in recent years, principally for political reasons. A discussion of this trend follows.

At the end of 1993, the CPC and Chinese Central Government launched a tax-revenue-division program.[217] According to the program, China's annual tax revenue has been split between central government and local governments using a new set of criteria. The implementation of this program has fundamentally altered the respective fiscal abilities of Chinese central and local governments. As statistics show, the ratio of fiscal income of central government to local government was 22/78 in 1978, and the ratio of fiscal expense was 28/72. By 2008, these ratios had shifted to 53/47 and 21/79.[218] Clearly, these two sets of data indicate that, following tax-revenue-division reform, Chinese local governments have been given a smaller piece of the tax-revenue cake, but have had to contribute more strength to make the cake bigger. Besides this unfavorable factor, the one-veto-all criteria of China's official promotion system, which means that a government leader can never get promoted if he fails to fulfil only one task assigned by a superior government, creates enormous tension among local governmental seniors. The combination of these two factors has provided local senior officials with strong incentives to seek out alternative ways to substantially increase local fiscal income, so as to successfully complete heavy tasks with which they are saddled by superior governments. Sales of state shares of local state-controlled listed companies is one such method, which is well applied by Chinese local governmental heads to raise fiscal funds in a rapid manner. Even though statistics regarding this practice in China are not currently available, some high-profile cases can be used to demonstrate its existence. The case of Huaxin Cement Corporation will be used as an example.[219]

Huaxin Cement Corporation is a cement manufacturer headquartered at Huangshi city in Hubei province, and which has been listed on the Shanghai Stock Exchange since 1994. The biggest shareholder in Huaxin Cement Corporation is Huaxin Group Corporation, which is wholly owned by the SASAC of Huangshi city. On 6 June 2011, Huaxin Cement Corporation issued a notice to the public to announce that Huaxin Group Corporation, as the majority shareholder, had sold 2.28 per cent of the stocks of Huaxin Cement Corporation in its hands since 24 May 2011. The money raised through this sale was to be used by the Huangshi municipal government to build social security houses for the poor living in the city.

The building of 26,309 social security houses was assigned to the Huangshi municipal government as a political task by the Hubei provincial government at the beginning of 2011. After accepting the task, the Huangshi municipal government made a promise to the Hubei provincial government that all the houses would be under construction by the end of June 2011. Unfortunately, the Huangshi municipal government did not have sufficient fiscal reserves to keep this promise. Therefore, it subsequently sold some of its shares in Huaxin Cement Corporation to mitigate its shortage of money and guarantee the timely construction of the houses.

The case of Huaxin Cement Corporation plausibly demonstrates that local governments are indeed selling out state shares of local state-controlled listed companies in China in order to lift their own fiscal abilities. An effect of this practice is that the concentrated ownership of local state-controlled listed companies has become somewhat dispersed. Particularly given that sales of state-owned land and use of governmental debts has been increasingly constrained by the Chinese Central Government,[220] the financial significance of the sales of state shares of local state-controlled listed companies for local government looks even greater. Accordingly, the concentrated ownership structures of local state-controlled listed companies will probably continue to be scattered, which will at least theoretically exert positive impacts on the creation of a venture-capital-friendly legal ecology in China in the future.

As Donald Clarke claimed, 'China's legal system cannot be understood apart from its history and that history – whether imperial or modern – is overwhelmingly a story of centrality of the state'.[221] It is also applicable to the concentrated ownership of state-controlled listed companies. Through a retrospective of the developmental history of state-controlled listed companies, we are able to easily understand that the origin of their concentrated ownership and the recent dispersion of their ownership are driven by political factors. In other words, by looking back at China's historical path, it becomes explicable that 'the policy of corporatization does not involve a renunciation by the state of its ambition to remain the direct owner of enterprises in a number of sectors',[222] because 'this ambition makes no sense if profits are the only objective'.[223] Using the evidence of state-controlled listed companies, it is obvious that this theory of politics is readily applicable in emerging and socialist China. Therefore, improving the ownership of state-controlled listed companies cannot be separated from Chinese political reform, since political determinants have always decided China's formation and change, and in turn influenced the appearance of the legal ecology which is preferable to Chinese domestic venture capital. A brief scan of political reform in China follows.

Political reform in China

Along with China's economic reform at the end of the 1970s, senior leaders of the CPC, such as Mr. Xiaoping Deng, also initiated political reform in China.[224] Prior to the 1990s, however, China's political reform focused mainly on eliminating the influences of Maoism and decentralizing power down to local governments.[225] During that period, a transformation of the role of governments in the economic arena was only slightly carried out, by adopting a contracting model in some SOEs. In 1992, the CPC first proposed the mission of establishing a market economy within its socialist regime in its Fourteenth National Delegate Conference.[226] Soon thereafter, a corporatization movement was conducted among traditional SOEs.[227] Through this movement, almost all SOEs have been corporatized and equipped with modern corporate governance institutions. However, this did not substantively change the role of governments as participants in microeconomic activities. The underlying orientation of governments was still 'economic involvement', but not 'public service'.[228]

In 2007, President Jintao Hu pointed out that the establishment of a public service government ought to be the next goal of China's political reform.[229] According to an official explanation, this kind of government is responsible for creating a fair and competitive environment for economic participants by offering premium public goods, such as laws and regulations.[230] In addition, a public service government is committed to providing a well-devised system to safeguard the lives of ordinary people.[231] Specifically, a public service government should fulfil four tasks. First, it should build a wide-ranging social security system and a market-oriented employment system.[232] Second, it should improve the quality and lower the costs of education, medical care, and cultural activities.[233] Third, it should protect the environment and develop infrastructure.[234] Fourth, it should maintain the safety and order of society as a whole.[235] Since then, this goal of building a public service government has provided a direction for the transformation of Chinese governments.

However, the establishment of a public service government will endanger the vested interests of local governments and the agencies affiliated to the Chinese Central Government, because it will definitely narrow the range of their powers. Consequently, this reform mission may be thwarted by the affected parties, who determine China's political path to a large degree. With this in mind, some may ask whether the determination of the political entrepreneurs or the might of traditional political forces will win out when they clash with one another in a Chinese context. The answer given by this book is that the former will triumph, even though the victory may be marginal. A persuasive piece of empirical evidence in favor of this prediction is China's reform itself.

As mentioned above, since the late 1970s, China has begun the transformation from a centrally planned economy to the market economy. Following Xiaoping Deng's inspection trip to the south of China in 1992, the goal of establishing a socialist market economy has been officially recognized and stipulated by the Constitution of the PRC and the Charter of the CPC.[236] This goal has twofold meanings. First, the development of a market economy in China must be within the framework of socialism, a system led solely by the CPC. Second, the establishment of a market economy is the primary concern of Chinese supreme leaders. They have been and will be striving to accomplish this goal by carrying out economic, political, and legal reforms.

China's successful approach to developing its market economy over the past 30 years has empirically demonstrated the feasibility of the goal of establishing a socialist market economy. On the one hand, it confirms that socialism is basically compatible with the market economy. On the other hand, it also shows Chinese supreme leaders' continuous determination to reform inefficient institutions to promote the building of a market economy If those Chinese supreme leaders who act as political entrepreneurs did not have an upper hand against the forces of obstruction, China would still be struggling in the mire of poverty and inefficiency. Therefore, in support of current Chinese supreme leaders and their successors acting as political entrepreneurs, it is believed that they will continue to push the goal of constructing a market economy further through institutional improvements within the socialist regime, among which the establishment of a public service government mentioned above is one.

As the establishment of a public service government develops incrementally in China, the divestiture of state-owned shares in Chinese state-controlled listed companies will accompany it accordingly. The two reform missions mentioned here will be achieved incrementally in China, with the presence of the friendly legal ecology for the development of Chinese domestic venture capital arriving gradually. No short-cut will be available to the stakeholders in this process.

Notes

[1] Edward B. Roberts and Charles E. Eesley, 'Entrepreneurial Impact: The Role of MIT – An Updated Report' (2011) 7, *Foundations and Trends in Entrepreneurship*, 64.

[2] Paul Gompers and Josh Lerner, 'The Venture Capital Revolution' (2001) 15, *The Journal of Economic Perspectives*, 146.

[3] Guanghua Yu, 'The Policy Implication of Comparative Studies on Venture Capital Markets' (2002) 4, *Jurists Review*, 14.

[4] Ronald J. Gilson, 'Engineering a Venture Capital Market: Lessons from the American Experience' (2003) 55, *Stanford Law Review*, 1068.

[5] Ibid., pp. 1094–1110.

[6] Ibid.

[7] The introduction of this movement is available at http://cpc.people.com.cn/BIG5/33837/2534775.html (accessed 18 April 2014).

[8] Ibid.

[9] Ibid.

[10] Shan Da, 'The Birth of the Chinese GEM' (2009) *Securities Times* (31 March).

[11] Ibid.

[12] Southcn, 'What Have We Learnt from the Failure of the China New Technology Venture Investment Corporation?' available at http://www.southcn.com/tech/special/fxtz/case/200403150917.htm (accessed 18 April 2014).

[13] Curtis J. Milhaupt, 'The Market for Innovation in the United States and Japan: Venture Capital and the Comparative Corporate Governance Debate' (1997) 91, *Northwestern University Law Review*, 874.

[14] Ibid.

[15] Ibid.

[16] An introduction to Facebook is available at http://en.wikipedia.org/wiki/Facebook (accessed 18 April 2014).

[17] Tao Jiang, 'The Developmental Path of Alibaba', available at http://www.iceo.com.cn/chuangye/61/2012/0227/242396.shtml (accessed 18 April 2014).

[18] China Venture Capital Research Institute Limited, 'The Collaboration between Ningxiahong and Venture Capital', available at http://www.chinavcpe.com/research/case/2005-06-30/07f47326ccbd9352.html (accessed18 April 2014).

[19] See n 10 above.

[20] Ibid.

[21] See n 12 above.

[22] The Introduction of the Torch Scheme is available at http://www.chinatorch.gov.cn/ (accessed 18 April 2014).

[23] It is available at http://www.people.com.cn/zixun/flfgk/item/dwjjf/falv/2/2-1-43.html (accessed 18 April 2014).

[24] Zizhan Pan et al., 'Nanshan Venture Capital Fund', available at http://wenku.baidu.com/view/fd23c00b6c85ec3a87c2c51c.html (accessed 18 April 2014).

[25] The Introduction of Jiangsu Govtor Capital Company is available at http://www.js-vc. com/ (accessed 18 April 2014).

[26] See n 4 above.

[27] Rob Dixon, John Ritchie, and Di Guo, 'The Impact of Governance Structure and Financial Constraints on Risk Tolerance of VCs: An Empirical Work on China's Venture Capital Industry', available at http://www.cass.city.ac.uk/emg/seminars/EMGpapers1stOct/ Dixon_Guo_Ritchie.pdf (accessed 18 April 2014).

[28] The Introduction of Focus Media is available at http://news.xinhuanet.com/newmedia/ 2005-07/25/content_3262127.htm (accessed 18 April 2014).

[29] The Introduction of Fortune Capital is available at http://finance.people.com. cn/n/2013/0201/c355192-20407342.html (accessed 18 April 2014).

[30] See n 27 above.

[31] China Venture Capital Research Institute Limited, *China Venture Capital Yearbook (2007)* (Beijing: Democracy and Construction Press, 2007), p. 107.

[32] Ibid.

[33] Ibid., p. 230; China Venture Capital Research Institute Limited, *China Venture Capital Yearbook (2008)* (Beijing: Democracy and Construction Press, 2008), p. 258.

[34] Ibid. (2007), p. 221; Ibid. (2008), p. 235.

[35] Paul Gompers and Josh Lerner, *The Venture Capital Cycle* (Massachusetts: The MIT Press, 2nd edn, 2004), p. 6–7.

[36] Robert P. Bartlett, 'Venture Capital, Agency Costs, and the False Dichotomy of the Corporation' (2006) 54, *UCLA Law Review*, 53.

[37] Paul A. Gompers, Josh Lerner, Margaret M. Blair, and Thomas Hellmann, 'What Drives Venture Capital Fundraising?' (1998) 1998, *Brookings Papers on Economic Activity-Microeconomics*, 149.

[38] See n 2 above, p. 146. In addition, 'institutional investors' hereinbefore refer solely to non-financial institutions. At that time, financial institutions in America were not pre-cluded from investing in VC firms, but few of them showed interest in this sector due to strong risk-aversion.

[39] Ibid.

[40] Ibid.

[41] See n 13 above, p. 881.

[42] Paul Gompers and Josh Lerner, 'The Use of Covenants: An Empirical Analysis of Venture Partnership Agreement' (1996) 39, *Journal of Law and Economics*; Paul Gompers and Josh Lerner, 'An Analysis of Compensation in the U.S. Venture Capital Partnership' (1999) 51, *Journal of Financial Economics*; James M. Poterba, 'How Burdensome Are Capital Gains Taxes? Evidence from the United States.' (1987) 33, *Journal of Public Economics*.

[43] Paul Gompers and Josh Lerner, 'Venture Capitalists and the Decision to Go Public' (1994) 35, *Journal of Financial Economics*, 293–295.

[44] See n 2 above, p. 146.

[45] See n 43 above, pp. 293–295.

[46] See n 37 above, p. 149.

[47] See n 35 above, pp. 10–11.

[48] See n 13 above, p. 880.

[49] Ibid., p. 881.

[50] Vladimir I. Ivanov and Ronald W. Masulis, 'Corporate Venture Capital, Strategic Alliances, and the Governance of Newly Public Firms', available at http://cei.ier.hit-u. ac.jp/Japanese/database/documents/WP2008-15.pdf (accessed 1 Nov 2012).

[51] John D. Lutsi, 'Pensions Turn to Long-Haul Venture Capital Funds to Raise Returns' (1995) 16, *Corporate Cashflow*, 36.

[52] *See* n 13 above, pp. 880–881.

[53] Eric C. Sibbitt, 'Law, Venture Capital, and Entrepreneurism in Japan: A Microeconomic Perspective on the Impact of Law on the Generation and Financing of Venture Businesses' (1998) 13, *Connecticut Journal of International Law*, 85–105.

[54] In China, the fundraising and exit of foreign venture capital is usually carried out abroad. This model is called 'two-end-outside' by Chinese venture capitalists. Recently, some commentators have argued that this model may be substantially changed by the ongoing financial crisis. However, as Nanpeng Shen, CEO of Sequoia Capital (China), pointed out in the 11th China VC Forum in June 2009, the 'two-end-outside' model has not been significantly altered even if several RMB funds have been established by foreign venture capital. In addition, Shen's statement also implies that the latest financial tsunami does not cause many difficulties for American venture capital raising money in the United States, which has been confirmed by Song Jin, Vice-chairman of Gotham Capital Management. The speech of Shen is available at http://money.163.com/09/0605/14/5B25BPQK00253DMT. html (accessed 19 April 2014); Xinhuanet, 'Wall Street Journal: Hedge Funds and Private Equity in the Context of Financial Crisis', available at http://news.xinhuanet.com/fortune/2009-03/30/content_11099567.htm (accessed 19 April 2014).

[55] China Review News, 'The Environments for RMB Funds Are Still Immature', available at http://www.chinareviewnews.com/doc/1007/0/4/5/100704590.html?coluid=7&kindid=0&docid=100704590 (accessed 19 April 2014).

[56] *See* n 13 above, pp. 892–894.

[57] Xi Long and Jie Sun, 'The Development of Pension Funds in the PRC' (2012) 26, *Democracy & Legal System*, 30–33.

[58] Ibid.

[59] Ibid.

[60] Ibid.

[61] Ibid.

[62] Ibid.

[63] Ibid.

[64] Ibid.

[65] Ibid.

[66] Ibid.

[67] Ge Long and Chaoming Ren, 'Three Yuan and the Pension Funds for Chinese Farmer' (2009) The China Youth Daily (7 September).

[68] Ibid.

[69] Ibid.

[70] Ibid.

[71] Available at http://www.ssf.gov.cn/web/NewsInfo.asp?NewsId=42 (accessed 19 April 2014).

[72] Department of Population and Employment Statistics of the National Bureau of Statistics and Department of Planning and Finance of Ministry of Labour and Social Security, *China Labour Statistical Yearbook* (Beijing: China Statistical Press, 2005), p. 575.

[73] Article 28 of the Provisional Regulation.

[74] Siwei Cheng, 'The Development Path of Chinese Commercial Banks', available at http://news.xinhuanet.com/theory/2008-04/23/content_8033716.htm (accessed 20 April 2014).

[75] Ibid.

[76] Ibid.

[77] The introduction of Bank of China is available at http://www.boc.cn/ (accessed 20 April 2014).

[78] The introduction of the Agricultural Bank of China is available at http://www.abchina.com/cn/ (accessed 20 April 2014).

[79] The introduction of China Construction Bank is available at http://www.ccb.com/cn/home/index.html (accessed 18 April 2014).

[80] The introduction of the Industrial and Commercial Bank of China is available at http://www.icbc.com.cn/icbc/ (accessed 18 April 2014).

[81] Ping Liu, He Wang, and Le Dou, 'The Overview of the 60-Year Development of the Chinese Insurance Sector' (2010) 8, *Journal of Hubei University of Economics*, 34.

[82] Ibid., pp. 34–35.

[83] Ibid., pp. 35–36.

[84] Ibid., pp. 36.

[85] People.CN, 'The Incident of the SSF Being Sued', available at http://finance.people.com.cn/n/2013/0524/c1004-21603305.html (accessed 20 April 2014).

[86] The introduction of Silicon Valley Bank is available at http://www.svb.com/ (accessed 18 April 2014).

[87] See n 35 above, pp. 6–7.

[88] See n 13 above, p. 885.

[89] Chengyu Liu and Yalun Yan, 'Analysis of the Organizational Forms of Venture Capital', available at http://www.is-law.com/OurDocuments/VC0002BE.pdf (last accessed 20 April 2014).

[90] George G. Triantis, 'Financial Contract Design in the World of Venture Capital' (2001) 68, *University of Chicago Law Review*, 305.

[91] Gregory G. Oehler, 'The Wider Implications of "Implicit" Contracts in Venture Capital Partnerships' (2005) 1, *NYU Journal of Law & Business*, 492–493.

[92] David Rosenberg, 'The Two "Cycles" of Venture Capital' (2003) 28, *The Journal of Corporation Law*, 421.

[93] Christopher Gulinello, 'Venture Capital Funds, Organizational Law, and Passive Investors' (2006) 70, *Albany Law Review*, 304.

[94] *See* n 92 above, p. 421. The limited partnership agreements entered into by venture capitalists and venture investors are typically subject to Delaware law. Pursuant to Article 17-303(a) of Limited Partnerships of Delaware, 'a limited partner is not liable for the obligations of a limited partnership unless he or she is also a general partner or, in addition to the exercise of the rights and powers of a limited partner, he or she participates in the control of the business', available at http://delcode.delaware.gov/title6/c017/sc03/index.shtml (accessed 18 April 2014).

[95] *See* n 93 above.

[96] *See* n 4 above, p. 1089.

[97] Ibid.

[98] David Rosenberg, 'Venture Capital Limited Partnerships: A Study in Freedom of Contract' (2002) 2002, *Columbia Business Law Review*, 365.

[99] Ronald J. Gilson, 'Globalizing Corporate Governance: Convergence of Form or Function' in Jeffrey N. Gordon and Mark J. Roe (ed), *Convergence and Persistence in Corporate Governance* (Cambridge: Cambridge University Press, 2004), p. 148.

[100] Ibid.

[101] *See* n 98 above, p. 377.

[102] The Research Centre of the People's University of China on the Development of Venture Capital, *China Venture Capital Yearbook (2002)* (Beijing: Democracy and Construction Press, 2003), p. 69.

[103] People's Daily Online, 'Foreign VCs Have Begun to Focus on RMB Funds and Their Whole Cycles Will Be Finished in China', available at http://finance.people.com.cn/BIG5/8215/115194/6831527.html (accessed 20 April 2014).

[104] See n 7 above, pp. 885–887.

[105] See n 5, p. 1074.

[106] Ibid.

[107] Ibid., p. 1079.

[108] Ibid., p. 1080.

[109] Ibid., p. 1083.

[110] William B. Bratton, 'Venture Capital on the Downside: Preferred Stock and Corporate Control' (2002) 100, *Michigan Law Review*, 897.

[111] Oliver Williamson, 'Corporate Governance' (1984) 93, *Yale Law Journal*, 1197–1230.

[112] See n 5, p. 1084.

[113] Ibid.

[114] See n 13, p. 887.

[115] Klaus M. Schmidt, 'Convertible Securities and Venture Capital Finance' (2003) 58, *Journal of Finance*, 1139.

[116] See n 13, p. 887.

[117] Ibid.

[118] Ibid.

[119] William A. Klein and John C. Coffee Jr, *Business Organization and Finance: Legal and Economic Principles*, 9th edn. (New York, Foundation Press 2004), pp. 290–291.

[120] See n 5 above, p. 1086.

[121] Pin Jiang, 'The Contemplation around Limited Partnership', available at http://www.civillaw.com.cn/article/default.asp?id=8085 (accessed 20 April 2014).

[122] Ibid.

[123] Ibid.

[124] Ibid.

[125] Ibid.

[126] Jintao Hu, 'The Speech in the National Scientific and Technological Meeting', available at http://politics.people.com.cn/BIG5/1024/4011536.html (accessed 20 April 2014).

[127] Yixun Yan, 'The Explanation to "The Partnership Enterprise Law of the People's Republic of China (Draft for Revise)"', available at http://vip.chinalawinfo.com/newlaw2002/SLC/SLC.asp?Db=lfbj&Gid=1090520821 (accessed 20 April 2014).

[128] Article 61 of the Revised Partnership Enterprise Law of the People's Republic of China. It says 'a limited partnership enterprise shall be established by not less than 2 but not more than 50 partners, unless it is otherwise provided by law. A limited partnership enterprise shall have at least 1 general partner'.

[129] Junhai Liu, 'It Is Necessary to Establish Limited Partnership', available at http://www.civillaw.com.cn/article/default.asp?id=8800 (accessed 20 April 2014).

[130] The interview was conducted in late 2008. The questions were aimed at all government venture capital in China. Thus, the interviewee's answers basically described the operation of government venture capital as a whole. It is undeniable that the operational model of government venture capital does not reflect the operation of privately held venture capital in China. However, given the fact that government venture capital represents the majority of Chinese domestic venture capital, its use of incentive mechanisms reflects, to a large degree, the profile of Chinese domestic venture capital in this regard.

[131] In practice, venture capital first lays down in the company's articles of association its registered capital payable to the portfolio company, which is equal to the amount of its first-stage financing. By offering the first round of financing, the portfolio company can

usually satisfy minimum requirements for the registered capital stipulated by Chinese company law, and is also financially able to achieve its first business goal. Once this first goal is accomplished, venture capital increases its registered capital in the company to help it achieve the second business goal by revising the articles of association and changing the record of its registered capital at the responsible Administration Bureau of Industry and Commerce.

[132] Justin Tan, Wei Zhang, and Jun Xia, 'Managing Risk in a Transitional Environment: An Exploratory Study of Control and Incentive Mechanisms of Venture Capital Firms in China' (2008) 46, *Journal of Small Business Management*, 270–271. In the cited article, the authors divide the sample of government venture capital studied into Chinese domestic venture capital and foreign venture capital, both of which operated in mainland China from 2000 to 2002. However, during the period concerned, Chinese domestic venture capital was almost synonymous with government venture capital. The article also indirectly confirms this by mentioning, on several occasions, how governments influenced the operation of the sample of government venture capital studied or by quoting venture capitalists, clearly stating that they worked for some companies included in the sample. Thus, it can be plausibly deduced that Chinese domestic venture capital in the cited article could, to a large degree, be interpreted as government venture capital. For an overview of the evolution of Chinese domestic venture capital, see Yanming Han, 'The Development of Venture Capital in China and Its Current Problems' (2009) 1, *China Technological Wealth*, 84–87.

[133] Yuxiao Wang and Xi Wang, 'Research of Venture Capital Staged Financing Strategy and Investment Performance' (2013) 19, *Science and Technology Management Research*, 201–204.

[134] Yi Tan, Hong Huang, and Haitian Lu, 'The Effect of Venture Capital Investment – Evidence from China's Small and Medium-Sized Enterprises Board' (2013) 51, *Journal of Small Business Management*, 138–157. According to this article, of 75 sample venture capital companies operating in China by the end of 2010, 73 were Chinese domestic venture capital established between 1996 and 2000, and the remaining two were foreign venture capital. Given that the period between 1996 and 2000 represented the first genuine developmental stage of the Chinese venture capital sector, characterized by the exclusive dominance of government venture capital, we have reason to believe that the majority of the 73 sample domestic venture capital companies in the cited research concerned government venture capital.

[135] Ibid., p. 154.

[136] Xueyong Zhang and Li Liao, 'VCs' Backgrounds, IPO Underpricing and Post-IPO Performance' (2011) 6, *Economic Research Journal*, 129.

[137] Baoshu Wang, 'It Is Important to Understand the Spirit of the New Company Law', available at http://www.civillaw.com.cn/article/default.asp?id=24654 (accessed 21 April 2014).

[138] Junhai Liu, 'Institutional Innovations of the New Company Law', available at http://www.civillaw.com.cn/article/default.asp?id=25323 (accessed 21 April 2014); Frank H. Easterbrook and Daniel R. Fischel, *The Economic Structure of Corporate Law* (Cambridge: Harvard University Press, 1991).

[139] Fuhua Liu, 'Preferred Stocks – An Alternative of the State's Ownership' (1998) 3, *Reform of Economic System*, 88–91; Zixiang Hu, 'A Feasibility Research on the Change of State-owned Stock to the Priority Stock' (1996) 3, *Jianghan Tribune*, 60–62; Xiaobo Feng and Huanchen Wang, 'Brief Research on the Application of Preferred Stocks in the Reduction of State-held Shares' (2001) 6, *Research on Economics and Management*,

43–45; Chunping Wang, 'The Conversion of State-held Stocks to Preferred Stocks – A New Way for the Reform of SOEs' (2002) 11, *Coal Economic Research*, 22–23.

[140] Ibid.

[141] *See* n 139 above.

[142] Ibid.

[143] Xiangjun Guo and Jianjun Liu, 'Interpreting "Interim Measures for the Administration of Startup Investment Enterprises"' (2006) 3, *Securities Market Herald*, 12.

[144] Available at http://www.ndrc.gov.cn/zcfb/zcfbl/zcfbl2005/t20051115_49928.htm (accessed 21 April 2014).

[145] Article 15 of the Interim Measures for the Administration of Startup Investment Enterprises says 'VCs may make investments by the way of stocks, preferred stocks and convertible preferred stocks on the basis of the agreement with venture enterprises'.

[146] Peizhong Gan, 'The Legal Analysis of Manager Stock Options' (2002) 20, *Journal of China University of Political Science and Law*, 49.

[147] The Fifteenth CPC Central Committee, 'Decisions on SOEs Reform', available at http://cpc.people.com.cn/GB/64162/71380/71382/71386/4837883.html (accessed 21 April 2014).

[148] Ibid.

[149] See n 146 above, p. 49.

[150] Ibid.

[151] Ibid.

[152] Shi Xin, 'NASDAQ: The Model of Growth Enterprise Markets' (2008) 1, *Shenzhen Stock Exchange*, 62.

[153] *See* n 98 above.

[154] *See* n 99 above.

[155] Currently, the NASDAQ consists of the NASDAQ Global Select Market, the NASDAQ Global Market, and the NASDAQ Capital Market. The NASDAQ Capital Market aims to provide listing services for small and medium-sized enterprises, especially those in the high technology field. Available at http://www.nasdaq.com/about/nasdaq_listing_req_fees.pdf (accessed 21 April 2014).

[156] Ibid. Even though they are updated from time to time by the NASDAQ, these rules always match the features of small-scale enterprises.

[157] Ibid.

[158] Pursuant to the Securities Exchange Act of 1934, 'if the exchange authorities certify to the Commission (the SEC) that the security has been approved by the exchange for listing and registration, the registration shall become effective thirty days after the receipt of such certification by the Commission (the SEC) or within such shorter period of time as the Commission may determine'.

[159] *See* n 152 above.

[160] Available at http://en.wikipedia.org/wiki/Dot-com_bubble (accessed 21 April 2014).

[161] Ibid.

[162] It is believed that the dot-com bubble reflected the shortcomings of continuous listing regulations by the NASDAQ.

[163] As analyzed in the third chapter, the funds of American venture capital operating in China are principally in the form of US dollars. Therefore, after harvesting, American venture capital must provide returns to its venture investors in the form of US dollars. If portfolio companies are listed on Chinese stock markets, American venture capital can obtain only RMB by selling their shares in the secondary market. Then, it must be converted to US dollars and transferred to venture investors outside China. However,

China always adopts stringent policies regarding foreign currency exchange and transfer. Hence, in order to avoid the potential hassles caused by Chinese foreign currency
policy, American venture capital generally chooses to list successful portfolio companies
on overseas GEMs located in jurisdictions with free and flexible policies concerning
foreign currency exchange and transfer. See China Venture Capital Research Institute
Limited, *China Venture Capital Yearbook (2006)* (Beijing: Democracy and Construction
Press, 2006), p. 371.

[164] Without using SPVs, Chinese domestic companies must file an application to be
listed on overseas stock markets with the CSRC. See 'Notice regarding the Overseas
Listings of Chinese Domestic Enterprises', promulgated by the CSRC on 14 April 1999,
available at http://vip.chinalawinfo.com/NewLaw2002/SLC/slc.asp?db=chl&gid=23191
(accessed 21 April 2014).

[165] For an overview of the SPV model used by American VCs in China, please visit http://
finance.sina.com.cn/stock/blank/hcsscq.shtml (accessed 21 April 2014).

[166] Ibid.

[167] Ibid.

[168] Ibid.

[169] Available   at   http://news.xinhuanet.com/fortune/2006-08/10/content_4944032.htm
(accessed 21 April 2014).

[170] Ibid., Article 11.

[171] Lihong Wu, 'A Primary Analysis on the Red Chip Model' (2007) 2, *Hebei Enterprises*,
56.

[172] *See* n 169 above.

[173] *See* n 171 above, pp. 55–56. In practice, the approval of the incorporation of foreign-
invested companies is a routine administrative issue for Chinese governments. So, it is
much more easily granted than the approval of takeover by SPVs by the Ministry of
Commerce.

[174] Sino-manager Online, 'The Mystery of Zhongwang's IPO', available at http://www.sino-
manager.com/200987_7517.html (accessed 21 April 2014).

[175] Interview with the venture capitalist of the provincial GVC.

[176] People's Daily Online, 'GEM: Promoting Innovation and Serving Economic
Development', available at http://big5.xinhuanet.com/gate/big5/news.xinhuanet.com/
fortune/2009-10/23/content_12304608.htm (accessed 21 April 2014).

[177] Shanghai Stock Exchange, 'The Introduction to the Shanghai Stock Exchange', available at http://www.sse.com.cn/sseportal/ps/zhs/sjs/jysjs.shtml (accessed 21 April 2014);
Shenzhen Stock Exchange, 'The Introduction to the Shenzhen Stock Exchange', available at http://www.szse.cn/main/aboutus/bsjs/bsjj/index.shtml (accessed 21 April 2014).

[178] In 1988, the amendment of the Constitution of the PRC officially recognized the legitimate status of privately-owned economies.

[179] Theoretically, listing standards should also have been discussed here as a tactic to protect
the interests of SOEs, similar to listing approval policies. In practice, however, for the
sake of superficial equality, the listing standards of the Chinese main boards are not able
to play that role. Therefore, it is ignored it in this chapter.

[180] Raobin Sun, 'Thinking about the Chinese Stock Issuance System' (2009) 4, *Internet
Fortune*, 58.

[181] Ibid.

[182] Ibid.

[183] Zhimin Geng, 'The Internal Mechanism Underlying the Evolution of Chinese Stock
Issuance Systems' (2007) 40, *Journal of Zheng Zhou University*, 76.

[184] Here, the incentives resulting from the control-based model include but are not limited to the better implementation of government policies, the increase of political achievements, and the satisfaction of private interests.

[185] See n 183 above.

[186] Guoqiang Dai, 'Exploring the Approval Systems of Stock Issuance' (2008) 8, *Special Zone Economy*, 36.

[187] Ibid.

[188] Ibid.

[189] Ibid.

[190] Ibid.

[191] See n 180 above.

[192] See n 186 above.

[193] See n 184 above. After the CSRC receives the requisite documents from candidate companies, it needs to solicit advice from provincial governments in the areas in which those companies are located. Thus, to a large degree, this procedure indirectly maintains the practice that local governments select listed companies. Available at http://www.csrc. gov.cn/n575458/n870705/n1333591/11360537.html (accessed 21 April 2014).

[194] Interview with the venture capitalist of the GVC.

[195] See n 31 above, p. 274; Ceocio Online, 'The Sports Meeting of Listing', available at http://www.ceocio.com.cn/12/93/124/312/24512.html (visited on 21 April 2014).

[196] Shenzhen Stock Exchange, 'The Implementation Plan of the Shenzhen Stock Exchange regarding the Establishment of the SME Board', available at http://www.szse.cn/main/ sme/sczy/ywgz/200405255828.shtml (accessed 21 April 2014).

[197] More than 80 per cent of listed companies on the SME Board are privately-held. See n 33 above, p. 362.

[198] Ibid.

[199] Ibid., p. 377.

[200] Article 33 of 'Provisional Administration Method regarding Listing Stocks by Means of Initial Public Offerings', available at http://www.gov.cn/ziliao/flfg/2006-05/18/ content_283660.htm (accessed 21 April 2014).

[201] Ibid.

[202] Ibid.

[203] Ibid.

[204] See n 33 above, p. 367. Here, it is believed that some scholars may argue that the number of venture-capital-backed listed companies on the SME Board is acceptable given the short history of the Chinese domestic venture capital industry. As an academic product, this book opposes this kind of attitude which attributes everything to time. Certainly, time can explain some things. However, as a research project, this book must also try to find out the more complicated institutional factors which determine the malfunctioning of the SME Board for the purposes of the smooth exit of Chinese domestic venture capital.

[205] Ibid., p. 364.

[206] Article 2 of the Company Law 2006.

[207] The CSRC, 'Notice regarding the Pilot Reform of Equity Division', available at http://big5. csrc.gov.cn/SuniT/www.csrc.gov.cn/n575458/n776436/n804935/n2466682/2652975. html (accessed 21 April 2014).

[208] Ibid.

[209] *See* n 200 above.

[210] Available at http://finance.sina.com.cn/stock/opengem/index.shtml (accessed 21 April 2014).

[211] Jincai Wang, 'The Legal Institution Construction for the Development of Chinese Venture Capital Industry' in Siwei Cheng (ed), *The Strategic Thinking on the Formation and Development of Chinese Venture Capital Industry* (Beijing: Democracy and Construction Press, 2002), p. 210.

[212] Available at http://www.nbd.com.cn/newshtml/20091030/20091030024557388.html (accessed 21 April 2014).

[213] Beijing Newspaper, 'Many VCs Hastily Approached Huaqi Digital Right after Its Application for Being Listed on the GEM', available at http://it.people.com.cn/GB/9335395.html (accessed 21 April 2014).

[214] Although it is impossible to obtain accurate figures for the number of venture-capital-backed companies which are eligible for listing on the GEM, we have reason to believe that this number must be larger than seven. Therefore, many authentic venture-capital-backed companies which are qualified to float on the GEM have not obtained this opportunity.

[215] Bin Chen, Jian She, Xiaojin Wang, & Jianqing Lai, 'Positive Research on the Development of Chinese Privately-held Listed Companies', available at http://www.szse.cn/main/files/2008/02/25/091811911155.pdf (accessed 21 April 2014); China Development Gateway, 'Overhaul of SOEs', available at http://cn.chinagate.cn/reports/2007-03/13/content_2369560.htm (accessed 21 April 2014).

[216] Available at http://finance.sina.com.cn/stock/y/20080811/07055185859.shtml (accessed 21 April 2014).

[217] State Council of the PRC, 'Decision on the Implementation of the Tax-Revenue-Division Program', available at http://news.xinhuanet.com/ziliao/2005-03/17/content_2709622.htm (accessed 21 April 2014).

[218] Available at http://finance.sina.com.cn/roll/20100724/01588356765.shtml (accessed 21 April 2014).

[219] Xiaojie Liu, 'The SASAC of Huangshi Sold Stocks for Security Houses', available at http://www.nbd.com.cn/articles/2011-06-23/577559.html (accessed 21 April 2014).

[220] The State Council, 'Notice on Regulating the Fundraising Companies of Local Governments', available at http://www.gov.cn/zwgk/2010-06/13/content_1627195.htm (accessed 21 April 2014).

[221] Donald Clarke, 'Lost in Translation? Corporate Legal Transplants in China', available at http://papers.ssrn.com/sol3/papers.cfm?abstract_id=913784 (accessed 21 April 2014).

[222] Donald C. Clarke, 'Corporate Governance in China: An Overview' 14, *China Economic Review*, 494. In the cited article, Professor Clarke questions the legitimacy and competency of governments' keeping ownership in enterprises. This research agrees with the stance advanced by Professor Clarke.

[223] Ibid.

[224] Xinjian Bao, 'China's Political Reform: Historical Experiences and Current Choices' (2009) 161, *Shandong Social Sciences*, 19–20.

[225] Ibid.

[226] Available at http://news.xinhuanet.com/ziliao/2003-01/20/content_697129.htm. (accessed 21 April 2014).

[227] The Fourteenth CPC Central Committee, 'Decisions on the Establishment of the Socialist Market Economy', available at http://www.people.com.cn/GB/shizheng/252/5089/5106/5179/20010430/456592.html (accessed 21 April 2014).

[228] Xiuze Chang, 'How Do We Establish a Public Servant Government?', available at http://theory.people.com.cn/GB/49150/49152/9369415.html (accessed 21 April 2014).

[229] Jintao Hu, 'Report to the Seventeenth CPC National Delegates' Conference', available at http://news.xinhuanet.com/newscenter/2007-10/24/content_6938568_5.htm (accessed 21 April 2014).

[230] *See* n 476 above.

[231] Ibid.

[232] Ibid.

[233] Ibid.

[234] Ibid.

[235] Ibid.

[236] See Article 15 of the Constitution of the PRC and the General Provisions of the Charter of CPC.

Bibliography

Bao, X. (2009). China's political reform: Historical experiences and current choices. *Shandong Social Sciences, 161.*

Bartlett, R. P. (2006). Venture capital, agency costs, and the false dichotomy of the corporation. *UCLA Law Review, 54.*

Beijing Newspaper. Many VCs hastily approached Huaqi digital right after its application for being listed on the GEM. Available at <http://it.people.com.cn/GB/9335395.html>.

Bratton, W. B. (2002). Venture capital on the downside: Preferred stock and corporate control. *Michigan Law Review, 100.*

Ceocio Online. The sports meeting of listing. Available at <http://www.ceocio.com.cn/12/93/124/312/24512.html>.

Chang, X. How do we establish a public servant Government? Available at <http://theory.people.com.cn/GB/49150/49152/9369415.html>.

Chen, B., She, J., Wang, X., & Lai J. Positive research on the development of Chinese privately-held listed companies. Available at <http://www.szse.cn/main/files/2008/02/25/091811911155.pd>.

Cheng, S. The development path of Chinese commercial banks. Available at <http://news.xinhuanet.com/theory/2008-04/23/content_8033716.htm>.

China Development Gateway. Overhaul of SOEs. Available at <http://cn.chinagate.cn/reports/2007-03/13/content_2369560.htm>.

China Review News. The environments for RMB funds are still immature. Available at <http://www.chinareviewnews.com/doc/1007/0/4/5/100704590.html?coluid=7&kindid=0&docid=10070459>.

China Venture Capital Research Institute Limited. The collaboration between Ningxiahong and venture capital. Available at <http://www.chinavcpe.com/research/case/2005-06-30/07f47326ccbd9352.html>.

China Venture Capital Research Institute Limited. (2006). *China venture capital yearbook (2006).* Beijing: Democracy and Construction Press.

China Venture Capital Research Institute Limited. (2007). *China venture capital yearbook (2007).* Beijing: Democracy and Construction Press.

China Venture Capital Research Institute Limited. (2008). *China venture capital yearbook (2008).* Beijing: Democracy and Construction Press.

Clarke, D. C. (2003). Corporate governance in China: An overview. *China Economic Review, 14.*

Clarke, D. C. Lost in translation? Corporate legal transplants in China. Available at <http://papers.ssrn.com/sol3/papers.cfm?abstract_id=913784>.

Da, S. (2009). The birth of the Chinese GEM. *Securities Times* (March 31).

Dai, G. (2008). Exploring the approval systems of stock issuance. *Speical Zone Economy, 8.*

Department of Population and Employment Statistics of the National Bureau of Statistics and Department of Planning and Finance of Ministry of Labour and Social Security. (2005). *China labour statistical yearbook.* Beijing: China Statistical Press.

Dixon, R., Ritchie, J., & Guo, D. The impact of governance structure and financial constraints on risk tolerance of VCs: An empirical work on China's venture capital industry. Available at <http://www.cass.city.ac.uk/emg/seminars/EMGpapers1stOct/Dixon_Guo_Ritchie.pdf>.

Easterbrook, F. H., & Fischel, D. R. (1991). *The economic structure of corporate law.* Cambridge: Harvard University Press.

Feng, X., & Wang, H. (2001). Brief research on the application of preferred stocks in the reduction of state-held shares. *Research on Economics and Management, 6.*

Gan, P. (2002). The legal analysis of manager stock options. *Journal of China University of Political Science and Law, 20.*

Geng, Z. (2007). The internal mechanism underlying the evolution of chinese stock issuance systems. *Journal of ZhengZhou University, 40.*

Gilson, R. J. (2003). Engineering a venture capital market: Lessons from the American experience. *Stanford Law Review, 55.*

Gilson, R. J. (2004). Globalizing corporate governance: Convergence of form or function. In J. N. Gordon & M. J. Roe (Eds.), *Convergence and persistence in corporate governance.* Cambridge: Cambridge University Press.

Gompers, P., & Lerner, J. (1994). Venture capitalists and the decision to go public. *Journal of Financial Economics, 35.*

Gompers, P., & Lerner, J. (1996). The use of covenants: An empirical analysis of venture partnership agreement. *Journal of Law and Economics, 39.*

Gompers, P., & Lerner, J. (1999). An analysis of compensation in the U.S. venture capital partnership. *Journal of Financial Economics, 51.*

Gompers, P., & Lerner, J. (2001). The venture capital revolution. *The Journal of Economic Perspectives, 15.*

Gompers, P., & Lerner, J. (2004). *The venture capital cycle* (2nd ed.). Massachusetts: The MIT Press.

Gompers, P. A., Lerner, J., Blair, M. M., & Hellmann, T. (1998). What drives venture capital fundraising? 1998 Brookings papers on economic activity-microeconomics.

Gulinello, C. (2006). Venture capital funds, organizational law, and passive investors. *Albany Law Review, 70.*

Guo, X., & Liu, J. (2006). Interpreting 'Interim Measures for the Administration of Startup Investment Enterprises'. *Securities Market Herald, 3.*

Han, Y. (2009). The development of venture capital in China and its current problems. *China Technological Wealth, 1.*

Hu, J. Report to the Seventeenth CPC National Delegates' Conference. Available at <http://news.xinhuanet.com/newscenter/2007-10/24/content_6938568_5.htm>.

Hu, J. The speech in the national scientific and technological meeting. Available at <http://politics.people.com.cn/BIG5/1024/4011536.html>.

Hu, Z. (1996). A feasibility research on the change of state-owned stock to the priority stock. *Jianghan Tribune, 3.*

Ivanov, V. I., & Masulis, R. W. Corporate venture capital, strategic alliances, and the governance of newly public firms. Available at <http://cei.ier.hit-u.ac.jp/Japanese/database/documents/WP2008-15.pdf>.

Jiang, P. The contemplation around limited partnership. Available at <http://www.civillaw.com.cn/article/default.asp?id=8085>.

Jiang, T. The developmental path of Alibaba. Available at <http://www.iceo.com.cn/chuangye/61/2012/0227/242396.shtml>.

Klein, W. A., & Coffee, J. C., Jr. (2004). *Business organization and finance: Legal and economic principles* (9th ed.). New York: Foundation Press.

Liu, C., & Yan, Y. Analysis of the organizational forms of venture capital. Available at <http://www.is-law.com/OurDocuments/VC0002BE.pdf>.

Liu, F. (1998). Preferred stocks – an alternative of the state's ownership. *Reform of Economic System*, 3.

Liu, J. Institutional innovations of the new company law. Available at <http://www.civillaw.com.cn/article/default.asp?id=25323>.

Liu, J. It is necessary to establish limited partnership. Available at <http://www.civillaw.com.cn/article/default.asp?id=8800>.

Liu, P., Wang, H., & Dou, L. (2010). The overview of the 60-year development of the Chinese insurance sector. *Journal of Hubei University of Economics*, 8.

Liu, X. The SASAC of Huangshi sold stocks for security houses. Available at <http://www.nbd.com.cn/articles/2011-06-23/577559.html>.

Long, G., & Ren, C. (2009). Three yuan and the pension funds for Chinese farmer. *The China Youth Daily* (September 7).

Long, X., & Sun, J. (2012). The development of pension funds in the PRC. *Democracy & Legal System*, 26.

Lutsi, J. D. (1995). Pensions turn to Long-haul venture capital funds to raise returns. *Corporate Cashflow*, 16.

Milhaupt, C. J. (1997). The market for innovation in the United States and Japan: Venture capital and the comparative corporate governance debate. *Northwestern University Law Review*, 91.

Oehler, G. G. (2005). The wider implications of 'Implicit' contracts in venture capital partnerships. *NYU Journal of Law & Business*, 1.

Pan, Z., et al. Nanshan Venture Capital Fund. Available at <http://wenku.baidu.com/view/fd23c00b6c85ec3a87c2c51c.html>.

People.CN The incident of the SSF being sued. Available at <http://finance.people.com.cn/n/2013/0524/c1004-21603305.html>.

People's Daily Online. Foreign VCs have begun to focus on RMB funds and their whole cycles will be finished in China. Available at <http://finance.people.com.cn/BIG5/8215/115194/6831527.html>.

People's Daily Online. GEM: Promoting innovation and serving economic development. Available at <http://big5.xinhuanet.com/gate/big5/news.xinhuanet.com/fortune/2009-10/23/content_12304608.htm>.

Poterba, J. M. (1987). How burdensome are capital gains taxes? evidence from the United States. *Journal of Public Economics*, 33.

Roberts, E. B., & Eesley, C. E. (2011). Entrepreneurial impact: The role of MIT – an updated report. *Foundations and Trends in Entrepreneurship*, 7.

Rosenberg, D. (2002). Venture capital limited partnerships: A study in freedom of contract. *Columbia Business Law Review*, 2002.

Rosenberg, D. (2003). The two 'Cycles' of venture capital. *The Journal of Corporation Law*, 28.

Schmidt, K. M. (2003). Convertible securities and venture capital finance. *Journal of Finance*, 58.

Shanghai Stock Exchange. The introduction to the Shanghai stock exchange. Available at <http://www.sse.com.cn/sseportal/ps/zhs/sjs/jysjs.shtml>.

Shenzhen Stock Exchange. The implementation plan of the Shenzhen stock exchange regarding the establishment of the SME board. Available at <http://www.szse.cn/main/sme/sczy/ywgz/200405255828.shtml>.

Shenzhen Stock Exchange. The introduction to the Shenzhen stock exchange. Available at <http://www.szse.cn/main/aboutus/bsjs/bsjj/index.shtml>.

Sibbitt, E. C. (1998). Law, venture capital, and entrepreneurism in Japan: A microeconomic perspective on the impact of law on the generation and financing of venture businesses. *Connecticut Journal of International Law*, 13.

Sino-manager Online. The mystery of Zhongwang's IPO. Available at <http://www.sino-manager.com/200987_7517.html>.

Southcn. What have we learnt from the failure of the China new technology venture investment corporation? Available at <http://www.southcn.com/tech/special/fxtz/case/200403150917.htm>.

State Council of the PRC. Decision on the implementation of the tax-revenue-division program. Available at <http://news.xinhuanet.com/ziliao/2005-03/17/content_2709622.htm>.

Sun, R. (2009). Thinking about the Chinese stock issuance system. *Internet Fortune, 4*.

Tan, J., Zhang, W., & Xia, J. (2008). Managing risk in a transitional environment: An exploratory study of control and incentive mechanisms of venture capital firms in China. *Journal of Small Business Management, 46*.

Tan, Y., Huang, H., & Lu, H. (2013). The effect of venture capital investment – evidence from China's Small and Medium-sized Enterprises Board. *Journal of Small Business Management, 51*.

The CSRC. Notice regarding the pilot reform of equity division. Available at <http://big5.csrc.gov.cn/SuniT/www.csrc.gov.cn/n575458/n776436/n804935/n2466682/2652975.htm>.

The Fifteenth CPC Central Committee. Decisions on SOEs reform. Available at <http://cpc.people.com.cn/GB/64162/71380/71382/71386/4837883.html>.

The Fourteenth CPC Central Committee. Decisions on the establishment of the socialist market economy. Available at <http://www.people.com.cn/GB/shizheng/252/5089/5106/5179/20010430/456592.html>.

The Research Centre of the People's University of China on the Development of Venture Capital. (2003). *Chinaventure capital yearbook (2002)*. Beijing: Democracy and Construction Press.

The State Council. Notice on regulating the fundraising companies of local governments. Available at <http://www.gov.cn/zwgk/2010-06/13/content_1627195.htm>.

Triantis, G. G. (2001). Financial contract design in the world of venture capital. *University of Chicago Law Review, 68*.

Wang, B. It is important to understand the spirit of the new company law. Available at <http://www.civillaw.com.cn/article/default.asp?id=24654>.

Wang, C. (2002). The conversion of state-held stocks to preferred stocks – a new way for the reform of SOEs. *Coal Economic Research, 11*.

Wang, J. (2002). The legal institution construction for the development of Chinese venture capital industry. In S. Cheng (Ed.), *The strategic thinking on the formation and development of chinese venture capital industry*. Beijing: Democracy and Construction Press.

Wang, Y., & Wang, X. (2013). Research of venture capital staged financing strategy and investment performance. *Science and Technology Management Research, 19*.

Williamson, O. (1984). Corporate governance. *Yale Law Journal, 93*.

Wu, L. (2007). A primary analysis on the red chip model. *Hebei Enterprises, 2*.

Xin, S. (2008). NASDAQ: The model of growth enterprise markets. *Shenzhen Stock Exchange, 1*.

Xinhuanet. Wall street journal: Hedge Funds and private equity in the context of financial crisis. Available at <http://news.xinhuanet.com/fortune/2009-03/30/content_11099567.htm>.

Yan, Y. The explanation to 'The Partnership Enterprise Law of the People's Republic of China (Draft for Revise)'. Available at <http://vip.chinalawinfo.com/newlaw2002/SLC/SLC.asp?Db=lfbj&Gid=1090520821>.

Yu, G. (2002). The policy implication of comparative studies on venture capital markets. *Jurists Review, 4*.

Zhang, X., & Liao, L. (2011). VCs' backgrounds, IPO underpricing and post-IPO performance. *Economic Research Journal, 6*.

Index

Note: Page numbers followed by '*t*' refer to tables.

A

Agricultural Bank of China, 32–36
Alibaba, 5–7, 9
American Research Development
  Corporation, 1

B

Bank of China, 32–36
Board Representation, 22–23, 46–49, 51–52

C

CDH Fund, 13–14
China Construction Bank, 35–36
China New Technology Venture Investment
  Corporation, 2, 9–11
China Securities Regulatory Committee, 16
Convertible Preferred Stocks, 22–23, 47,
  49–52

D

Digital Equipment Corporation, 1, 25
Department of Labor, 25–26

E

Employee Retirement Income
  Security Act, 1, 25–26
Entrepreneurs, 3, 13–16, 22–23, 45–47, 55,
  65–66
External Innovation, 3, 9

F

Facebook, 3–5, 9
Focus Media, 16–18
Fortune Capital, 18–20

G

GEM, 18, 22–23, 54–55, 57, 59–61
Great Leap Movement, 38

H

High Risks, 19, 25, 46–47
High Technology Zones, 11–13

I

Industrial and Commercial Bank of China,
  32–33, 36–37
In-house Innovation, 3

J

Jiangsu Govtor Capital Company, 14–16
Jintao Hu, 65

K

Kenneth Olsen, 1

L

Limited Partnership, 22–23, 26, 45–48, 51–53

M

Main Boards, 18, 22–23, 53, 55–60

N

Nanshan Venture Capital Fund, 13–14
National Association of Securities Dealers
  Automated Quotations, 53
Ningxiahong, 7–9

O

Organizational Arrangements, 45

P

Partnership Enterprise Law of
  the PRC, 47–48
Pension Funds, 1, 22–23, 25–32, 27*t*, 31*t*, 41
Political Reform, 51–52, 64–66
Prudent Man, 1, 25–26

Q

Qiuyun Long, 18

R

Reputation, 5–6, 10–11, 19, 41,
    54–55

S

Silicon Valley Bank, 42
SME Board, 22–23, 55, 57–61, 58t, 59t
Social Security Fund, 30, 31t, 32, 41

Staged Financing, 22–23, 46–49, 51–52
Startups, 3–4, 10–15, 42–43
State-owned Enterprises, 1–2
Stock Options, 22–23, 46–47, 50–52

T

Tax-revenue-division Program, 63–64
Torch Scheme, 9–13

U

Unemployment Insurance, 30, 31t

Printed in the United States
By Bookmasters